I0816201
AN
UNHOLY
ALLIANCE

AN UNHOLY ALLIANCE

How Progressivism Brought About an Islamist Invasion

MICHAEL YOUSSEF

Ascaine Press

AN UNHOLY ALLIANCE:
How Progressivism Brought About an Islamist Invasion

Library of Congress Control Number: 2025927001

Paperback ISBN: 979-8-89317-704-6
Ebook ISBN: 979-8-89317-705-3

Published by Ascaine Press, a publishing imprint of Global Publishing Partners, LLC, Nashville, TN. www.GlobalPublishingPartners.com

Published in association with Don Gates of the literary agency: The Gates Group, www.the-gates-group.com

Printed in the USA.

26 27 28 29 30 31 32 33 34 ShM 10 9 8 7 6 5 4 3 2

CONTENTS

PROLOGUE

AFTER SATURDAY, SUNDAY

On Wednesday evening, May 21, 2025, a gunman approached the Capital Jewish Museum in Washington, D.C., and unleashed a hail of bullets at a thirty-year-old Israeli man, Yaron Lischinsky, and his twenty-six-year-old Jewish-American girlfriend, Sarah Milgrim. He reloaded, then shot the young woman execution-style as she tried to crawl away.

When police examined the body of Yaron Lischinsky, they found an engagement ring in his pocket. He was planning to take Sarah Milgrim to Jerusalem in a few days to introduce her to his parents and propose to her. The couple had met while working at the Israeli Embassy in Washington.

Yaron Lischinsky was a devout Christian. Raised in both Israel and Germany by a Jewish father and a Christian mother, he spoke German, Hebrew, English, and Japanese. He would often engage with friends in hours-long conversations about Christian theology. One of Lischinsky's Christian friends, Mariam Wahba, said that Lischinsky "didn't just want to understand the world. He wanted to mend it."[1]

The lives of Yaron Lischinsky and Sarah Milgrim were cut short by a radical gunman shouting, "Free, free Palestine!" and "I did this for Gaza!"

What kind of man was the killer? He was neither a Muslim nor a Palestinian, as you might expect. He was an American-born Progressive activist from Chicago who had been radicalized by leftist propaganda. For years, he had been active in the Chicago protest scene, usually ranting about the police and big corporations.[2]

Why would an activist of the Progressive left adopt the murderous passions of a radical Islamist? On the surface, it seems to make no sense. After all, the most cherished causes of the Progressive left include equal rights for women and social acceptance for gays, lesbians, and transgender people. On these issues, Progressives and Islamists are 100 percent opposed to each other. Yet the Progressive left has adopted the Islamist Palestinian cause as its own. How is this possible?

In fact, the murderer of Yaron Lischinsky and Sarah Milgrim exemplifies the devil's bargain between radical Islam and radical Progressivism. In the coming pages, I'll show you how this unholy alliance came to be—and what it means for our future.

A CIVILIZATION UNDER ASSAULT

Our civilization is under assault from radical, political Islam. And our civilization is under assault from the radical, secular left. Both of these movements seek our submission and our destruction—and they have joined forces.

Radical, political Islam is bent on sweeping away Western civilization and imposing a global caliphate. The radical Progressive left is bent on sweeping away Western civilization and imposing a Marxist paradise, without "capitalism," without "colonialism," and without Christianity and the nuclear family. The Islamists and the leftists have bonded over their shared hatred of Western Judeo-Christian values.

There is a proverb among radical Islamists: "First the Saturday people, then the Sunday people"—or more simply, "After Saturday, Sunday." This means that, after those who worship on Saturday (the Jews) are eliminated, those who worship on Sunday (the Christians) will be next. Radical Islamism, which has long threatened our civilization from the far side of the globe, has now spread its tentacles throughout our society. The threat is no longer "over there"—it's *here.*

The goal of radical Islamism is to build a seventh-century global caliphate atop the rubble of our civilization.

We are under a combined assault from Islamists and leftists—and our leaders are either too afraid or too passive to confront the threat. These two ideologies reject peaceful coexistence with the rest of the world and demand the complete submission of their enemies. As Christianity withers in many corners of Europe and America, the radicals scurry into the vacuum. In Germany, France, the United Kingdom, and America, enclaves of unassimilated Muslims are springing up and radical leftists are seizing political power.

But there is hope. I have written this book as a wake-up call for the Christian Church—and for all of Western society. There is work you and I *can* do—work we *must* do—to preserve our Judeo-Christian heritage and our civilization for generations to come.

Would you like to know more? Would you like to hear about the hope I have for the future of our society? Then roll up your sleeves, turn the page, and let's get started.

1

THE RED-GREEN OMNICAUSE

In 2019, *Time* magazine named sixteen-year-old climate activist Greta Thunberg its "Person of the Year"—the youngest person ever to be so honored.[3]

When Greta Thunberg reached her early twenties, she turned her attention to a new cause: Palestinians in Gaza. In May 2024, seven months after Hamas killed, raped, and kidnapped hundreds of Israelis in the October 7 invasion, Thunberg wrapped herself in a black-and-white Hamas keffiyeh and protested at the Eurovision Song Contest in Malmö, Sweden. "Shame on you!" she shouted, angered by contest organizers for letting an Israeli singer perform.

In response, the humanitarian organization Stop Antisemitism labeled Thunberg "antisemite of the week." Liora Rez, the group's founder, said, "Greta's hatred of the world's only Jewish nation eclipses her love of the environment. Despite Israel being a global leader in tackling climate disasters and rushing to aid in crises worldwide, Greta sides with their homicidal terrorist enemies."[4]

In June 2025, Thunberg traveled to Sicily and boarded a 59-foot sailboat, the *Madleen*, along with activists from other countries. Their stated goal was to slip through Israel's naval blockade and deliver humanitarian aid to people in Gaza. The *Madleen* was quickly intercepted and the passengers were taken to the Israeli port of Ashdod.[5] Israeli authorities called the *Madleen* a "selfie yacht" engaged in "Instagram activism." The Israelis noted that the boat's cargo amounted to "less than a single truckload of aid."[6]

Israeli Defense Minister Israel Katz ordered Thunberg and her shipmates to a screening room to watch a video. The video began rolling—and Thunberg and her friends realized it was video footage shot by Hamas terrorists during their murder spree on October 7, 2023. Thunberg and the other activists rushed out of the room, refusing to watch the video.

Katz said, "The antisemitic flotilla members are turning a blind eye to the truth and have proven once again that they prefer the murderers to the murdered and continue to ignore the atrocities committed by Hamas."[7]

I don't blame Greta Thunberg for being morally confused. By all accounts, she has been well indoctrinated but poorly educated. After viewing a climate-change video in the fifth grade, she went into a deep depression. She stopped eating, speaking, and playing the piano. She was diagnosed with autism and obsessive-compulsive disorder. At age fifteen, she skipped school to protest in front of the Swedish parliament building.[8]

Now that Greta Thunberg is an internationally known climate activist, it's not surprising that other woke activists would want to exploit her fame for their own benefit. I genuinely feel sorry for her. Radical activists have hijacked her passion to "save the planet" and have twisted it into genocidal hatred. She's been captured by a mindset that fuses every secular-left cause into a single concoction of misguided activism.

This mindset is called "the Omnicause."

UNDERSTANDING THE OMNICAUSE

The term "Omnicause" was created by Iowa accountant Alysia Ames. In her X.com profile, she writes, "I coined the term 'omnicause' in frustration with the left pretending every cause is actually the same thing because I want the left to be smart and win!"[9]

British journalist Hadley Freeman explains the Omnicause this way: "The Omnicause is, simply, every cause you must care about if you're A Good Progressive, rolled into one, because everything in the world is connected. So trans rights are connected to

Palestinian rights are connected to environmental concerns, and any self-respecting progressive who cares about one has to care about the other two."[10]

When we watch the news, we may see protesters with signs that read "Gays for Gaza!" or "Queers for Palestine!" And we can't help thinking, "Don't these protesters know that Hamas would happily torture and kill them because of their homosexuality?"

In 2016, Hamas tortured and executed Mahmoud Ishtiwi, the commander of Hamas's fierce Zeitoun battalion, over unproven accusations that he was a practicing homosexual.[11] If a top Hamas general can be brutally executed on the mere *suspicion* of being gay, what chance would a "queer" campus protester from America have in Gaza?

But don't expect logic from those captured by the Omnicause. Yes, the alliance between the radical left and radical Islamists is irrational. Yes, it causes gay people to side with Islamists who would kill them as soon as look at them. Yes, it causes feminists to side with Hamas terrorists who have murdered and raped Israeli women.[12] But these internal contradictions don't bother those who are dedicated to the Omnicause.

In 2024, *The Wall Street Journal* opinion writer Andy Kessler penned a column headlined, "The 'Omnicause' Is Collapsing." He wrote, "Did I see climate warrior Greta Thunberg wearing a kaffiyeh? Sure enough. . . Welcome to the Omnicause. If you protest one thing, you protest everything—intersectional inanity. Like 'Queers for Palestine,' which makes as much sense as 'Chickens for KFC.' Fortunately, the Omnicause is beginning to collapse under the weight of its logical fallacies."[13]

I'm afraid Mr. Kessler's optimism is mere wishful thinking. The evidence shows that, if anything, the Omnicause is growing bigger, more vocal, and more extreme in its views.

In June 2024, one of the most bizarre events in human history took place on the streets of Philadelphia: Kaffiyeh-wearing pro-Palestine marchers collided with a rainbow-banner-waving Pride March. Gay marchers proclaiming "Love, Unity, and Visibility" on their shirts seemed baffled by hostile people holding signs reading,

"Long Live the Intifada!" and "Kill Hostages Now!"[14] The absurdity of this scene would be hilarious if it were not so tragic.

The Omnicause will never collapse under the weight of its logical fallacies, because leftist and Islamist ideologies don't care about logic. No less an authority than the Smithsonian National Museum of African American History and Culture has declared that "objective, rational, linear thinking" is a "white value" to be distrusted and rejected.[15] Unreasoning passion and emotion drive the Omnicause—not logic.

THE RED-GREEN ALLIANCE

Journalist Eli Lake, host of the *Breaking History* podcast, uses a different term to describe the Omnicause: the Red-Green Alliance. "Red" refers to the political left, including Progressives, Socialists, and Communists. "Green" is the color most closely associated with Islam and is commonly seen on its flags and banners. The term "Red-Green Alliance" refers to the paradoxical coalition between the secular left and fundamentalist Islamists who have bonded over their shared hatred for Western, Judeo-Christian values.

To illustrate this strange marriage between Islamists and Western leftists, Lake cites this example: "The Democratic Socialists of America simultaneously support making New York a national hub for transgender youth medicine but also want to globalize the intifada [rebellion]. It supports the bleeding edge of social progressive values while throwing its full support behind the fanatic fascists who filmed their mass murder of Jews and proudly posted the videos to Telegram."

Lake traces the origins of the "cognitively dissonant" Red-Green Alliance to the Iranian revolution of 1978 and 1979. Leftist journalists and politicians fawned over the exiled Ayatollah Ruhollah Khomeini, who seemed poised to replace the authoritarian (but pro-Western) Shah of Iran. Receiving reporters at his home-in-exile in France, the Ayatollah sat cross-legged under an apple tree and gave scores of media interviews. Leftist reporters, seeing and hearing only what would confirm their biases, portrayed the Ayatollah as (in Lake's words) "a pious democrat, perhaps even a progressive figure."

Andrew Young, President Jimmy Carter's UN ambassador, predicted that the Ayatollah would go down in history as "a saint."

Any of these journalists or government officials could have read the Ayatollah's 1970 book *Islamic Government*, which spelled out his hatred of the West, his loathing for democracy, and his desire to impose Sharia law on the world. But no one bothered to read it.[16] When the Shah fell and the Ayatollah came to power, he plunged Iran into a dystopian nightmare of oppression, mass executions, the subjugation of women, and more.

When the aggressive ambitions of the Islamists meet the wishful thinking of the secular left, the result is a Red-Green Alliance, an intersectional Omnicause that leads the world down a path of enslavement, destruction, and death.

A SHARED HATE

The term "Omnicause" may be new, but the Omnicause mindset is a very old idea. At many times and in many regions of the world, leftist movements have sprung up and called themselves "Popular Front" movements. These range from the Spanish Popular Front of the 1930s to the Popular Front for the Liberation of Palestine today. A Popular Front movement is an alliance of dissimilar causes that join together to defeat a common enemy. A slogan often heard in Popular Fronts is "No enemies to the left, no friends to the right."[17]

Famed American journalist Whittaker Chambers wrote in his book *Witness* about his time in the Communist Party in the 1920s and 1930s, before he became disillusioned by Stalin and Soviet Communism. He wrote that when people became captured by the Popular Front mindset, they could no longer see reality as it is because they had "substituted the habit of delusion" and they "became hysterical whenever the root of their delusion" was brought to light.

"The Popular Front mind," Chambers wrote, ". . . told the nation what it should believe; it made up the nation's mind for it. The Popular Fronters had made themselves the 'experts.' They controlled the narrows of news and opinion. . . . The nation heard in their fatal errors the voice of those having authority."[18]

Whether you call it the Omnicause or the Red-Green Alliance or the Popular Front mind, the self-contradictory leftist mentality maintains its perverse grip on America and across the Western world. The "fatal errors" of the Popular Front mind have tightened their stranglehold on "the narrows of news and opinion," as well as our universities, many of our most influential corporations, and all levels of most Western governments. That's why our universities, news media, and other elite power centers are much farther to the left than the culture.

It makes no rational sense for feminists and LGBTQ activists to ally themselves with radical Islamists—yet they do, and they see no contradiction. They are in the grip of the delusion of the Omnicause, the psychosis of the Popular Front mind. The secular left and radical Islamists have one thing in common: shared hate. Both hate Christianity. Both hate the Jews and the State of Israel. Both hate Judeo-Christian morality. Both hate the United States. Both hate Western civilization. They ignore their irreconcilable differences because of their shared hate.

I remember marveling when the Progressive Left made a patron saint out of Linda Sarsour, a radical Islamist who advocates Sharia law for American society. In 2015, *The New York Times* published an effusive profile of Sarsour, calling her the "Brooklyn homegirl in a hijab."[19] The *Times* piece neglected to mention that Sarsour's pro-Sharia advocacy is completely opposed to American democracy, First Amendment freedoms, human rights, feminism and equality for women, and just about every other cause Progressives hold dear.

As I write these words, we are witnessing the merger of the Progressive left with radical Islamism in an election for the control of one of the greatest cities in the world—New York City.

JIHAD BY DEMOCRACY

On November 4, 2025, New York City voters chose thirty-four-year-old Zohran Mamdani as the mayor of New York City. A member of the far-left Democratic Socialists of America, the aggressively anti-capitalist, anti-Western Mamdani became the chief executive of the most important hub of finance and commerce in the Western world. Born in Uganda of Indian Muslim parents, Mamdani immigrated to the United States at a young age. He attended Bowdoin College in Brunswick, Maine, where he cofounded the first Students for Justice in Palestine (SJP) chapter on that campus. (The Anti-Defamation League and other Jewish advocacy groups have accused SJP of promoting anti-Semitism.[20])

Zohran Mamdani is a practicing Twelver Shia Muslim.[21] What does that mean?

Islam is divided into several sects, most notably the Sunni and Shia sects. Twelver Shiism is the largest branch of Shia Islam, and is defined by its belief in twelve divinely ordained Imams (rightful successors to Muhammad). Twelver Shia Islam is the most extreme, anti-Western branch of Islam, and it is the official state religion of Iran.

In his public statements, Mamdani downplays his own Twelver beliefs. He achieved victory by shrewdly wrapping the poison pill of Islamism in a sugar-coating of "free" giveaways and socialist income redistribution: taxing millionaires and billionaires, freezing rents, establishing government-run grocery stores, providing free childcare and bus transportation, defunding the police, opposing Immigration and Customs Enforcement (ICE), and more.[22]

Mamdani's father, a political science professor at Columbia University, specializes in "decolonization studies." Zohran spent most of his life absorbing his father's far-left, Marxist views. His policy statements come straight from the anti-Western doctrines of "Third-Worldism," which is rooted in grievances against formerly colonial nations.

Zohran Mamdani's well-documented hostility toward Israel is partly explained by this mindset. Third-Worldists divide the world into oppressors and the oppressed. Jews have been persecuted and oppressed by the Babylonians and Assyrians in Old Testament times, the Romans in New Testament times, and the Nazis during the Holocaust. Yet Third-Worldists irrationally treat the Jews as "oppressors." Though the Jews are indigenous to Israel, Third-Worldists call Jews who return to their ancient homeland "colonizers."

Mamdani won by pandering to voters too young to understand the horrors of socialism. I grew up in Egypt under the Islamo-socialist regime of Gamal Abdel Nasser, chairman of the Revolutionary Command Council of Egypt. His military-socialist dictatorship controlled every aspect of our lives. I couldn't wait to escape from Egypt and find freedom in the West. I wish I could share my firsthand knowledge of socialism with Mamdani's voters.

One of Mamdani's winning strategies was to stoke his voters' suspicions that the system was rigged against them by the rich and powerful. Asked on NBC's *Meet the Press* if "billionaires have a right to exist," he replied, "I don't think that we should have billionaires because, frankly, it is so much money in a moment of such inequality. And ultimately, what we need more of is equality across our city and across our state and across our country."[23]

To people who don't know any better, Mamdani's "no billionaires" goal sounds perfectly reasonable. Who could argue against "equality"? But Russian chess master Garry Kasparov grew up under socialism in the Soviet Union, and he observed, "Capitalism's unequal distribution of prosperity is far better than socialism's equal distribution of misery."[24]

Zohran Mamdani is the embodiment of the strange union of radical Islamism and radical far-left Progressivism. During his campaign, Mamdani refused to say whether he believes Israel has a right to exist, and he refused to distance himself from the phrase "Globalize the intifada"—a rallying cry associated with murder and violence against Jews around the world.[25]

After Mamdani won the Democratic primary, his supporters at victory parties around the city chanted, "Globalize the intifada!" Mohammed el-Kurd, the Palestinian correspondent for the far-left magazine *The Nation*, tweeted his election-night thoughts about Mamdani's victory: "Consider the intifada globalized."[26]

THE *TAQIYYA* DOCTRINE

During Zohran Mamdani's *Meet the Press* interview after the election, an NBC host asked him, "Do you condemn that phrase,

'Globalize the intifada'?" He adroitly fended off the question, saying, "That's not language that I use. The language that I use . . . [is] grounded in a belief in universal human rights. . . . I don't believe that the role of the mayor is to police speech."[27]

Mamdani's clever answer is what political observers call a "dog whistle"—a subtly crafted political message that sounds reasonable to most voters but conceals a hidden message that only Mamdani's Islamist voters can hear. He is tacitly telling them, "You know I can't openly support violence against Jews, but when I refuse to condemn it, you know I'm one of you."

An Islamic doctrine called *taqiyya* (meaning "prudence" or "concealment") permits a Muslim to deceive his enemies until he gains the upper hand. While I can't look into Mamdani's heart and judge his motives, his Twelver Shia belief system clearly permits deception in order to get elected. In fact, as former Muslim, Imtiaz Mahmood explains that *taqiyya* "glorifies and sanctifies falsehood as a moral duty. . . . Western people have a hard time accepting that such a thing is possible, despite it being as basic to Islam as charity is to Christianity."[28]

Amjad Taha is a political analyst from the United Arab Emirates (UAE) who warns that Islamists are waging jihad (struggle) against the West by using our democracy against us. Soon after Zohran Mamdani won the New York City mayoral primary, Taha posted on X, "When a Muslim Brotherhood-influenced, Marxist-flavored politician becomes mayor of a once civilized city, that's not democracy; it's like handing the keys of Solomon's Temple to Nebuchadnezzar and expecting a prayer service. . . . If New York has truly fallen, if Zohran Mamdani becomes mayor, prepare to watch churches turn into jihadist campuses."[29]

Days before Mamdani's election, Taha warned that Islamists had also used democracy to gain control of other countries. He posted, "Democracy is not a universal solution. Yes, democracy has its merits, but it also has serious flaws. One of them is that, under its name, Islamist extremists and Muslim Brotherhood terrorists can become prime ministers or congressmen. . . . When democracy was tried in Gaza, it gave power to Hamas. In Egypt, it brought the Muslim

Brotherhood. In Libya, it handed the country to militias. . . . If your version of democracy empowers terrorists, then your system is not enlightened, it is infected."[30]

USEFUL BUT IGNORANT

The Russian revolutionary Vladimir Lenin is said to have coined the term "useful idiot" to describe people who are easily manipulated into thinking they are fighting for a noble cause. He saw such people as unwitting tools to accomplish his goals. By the time they realized they had been duped, it would be too late. Lenin's "useful idiots" were usually executed when they ceased to be "useful."

I don't like the term "useful idiot" to describe passionate young activists like Greta Thunberg, because she's definitely *not* an idiot. She's intelligent and articulate—but she's woefully misguided and indoctrinated. In fact, many of the kaffiyeh-clad activists protesting on campuses across the country have only a vague notion of what they are shouting about. As UnHerd columnist Mary Harrington observed, many young protesters are "mostly there for the vibe."[31]

An online video shows protesters at New York's Columbia University chanting, "From the River to the Sea, Palestine will be free!"—a slogan that calls for the elimination of all Jews from the land of Israel. In the video, a reporter stops one of the protesters, a young woman, and asks, "What does 'from the River to the Sea' mean?"

The protester exuberantly replies, "It means that Palestine should be free. It should be autonomous."

"What river?"

The young woman looks perplexed—and a little shaken. "Um—okay. That expression is not anything—"

"No," the reporter presses, "there's an actual river and an actual sea."

"Yeah, I'm aware. Um—"

"But what river, what sea?"

"That river that literally, um, is beside Israel and the Palestinian territories."[32]

Clearly, this intelligent, articulate young woman has no idea that the phrase she's been chanting refers to the land between the Jordan River and the Mediterranean Sea—and the chant is a code for genocide.[33]

Another online video shows two anti-Israel activists, both college-age women, being interviewed during a noisy protest at New York University. The interviewer asks one of the young women to explain the goal of the NYU demonstration.

The protester says, "I think the main goal is just showing our support for Palestine and demanding that NYU stop—" She pauses and gropes for words—then confesses, "I honestly don't know all of what NYU is doing."

The interviewer asks, "Is there something that NYU is doing wrong?"

"I really don't know. I'm pretty sure they're—" She pauses again, grimacing with embarrassment, and turns to her friend. "Do you know what NYU is doing?"

"About what?"

"About Israel. Why are we protesting—here at NYU specifically?"

The friend shrugs and says, "I wish I was more educated."[34]

I agree! I wish these two passionate young college students were more educated. Sadly, they have been indoctrinated instead. They are intelligent young women attending an elite university, but they have been duped into the role of "useful idiots."

Our civilization is infected by two toxic ideologies that have joined forces. In their shared hatred for Western values, the secular left and radical Islamists have forged an unholy alliance. Looked at logically, their alliance seems doomed to collapse under the weight of its internal contradictions. But once you understand that these two movements are united by a shared hate and a common enemy, their alliance makes diabolical sense.

In the coming pages, we will see example after example of this unholy alliance changing the face of Western democracies and threatening Western civilization.

2

THE OCCUPATION HAS BEGUN

In March 2025, Andre Sayegh, the mayor of Paterson, New Jersey, declared his city "the capital of Palestine in the United States of America" and "the fourth holiest city in the world" after Mecca, Medina, and Jerusalem. Sayegh became Paterson's first Arab-American mayor when he was elected by a landslide in 2018. With an estimated 30,000 Muslims in a city of more than 150,000 people, Muslims are hardly a majority, but they do make up a sizable minority group in the city.[35]

Mayor Sayegh, the son of a Syrian mother and a Lebanese father, is not himself a Muslim but a practicing Catholic. For a Christian mayor to declare his city to be a Muslim holy city seems more than bizarre—it seems like an act of submission to Islam. The mayor's remarks seemed especially ill timed because he made them while Israel and Hamas were at war in Gaza—and his words could easily be interpreted as taking the side of Hamas.

A Paterson street was renamed "Palestine Way" in 2022, and the district around the street is officially known as "Little Palestine." As one observer wrote, "Critics argue that the city's transformation into an Islamic and Palestinian enclave could undermine the values that have traditionally defined Paterson. As Paterson continues to evolve, the city's identity remains a contentious issue, with Muslim leaders asserting their political and religious influence and others raising concerns about the implications for the broader community."[36]

I can't read Mayor Sayegh's mind, but it's possible he believes that, as a politician, he must bend the knee to an increasingly powerful pressure group—the Islamist community. Amil Imani, an Iranian-American writer and political analyst, has suggested two appropriate labels for the growing political and social pressure that Islamists are flexing in Western civilization today: "Soft Jihad" or "Stealth Jihad."

In early 2020, Imani attended a closed fund-raising event at the Hyatt Regency Hotel in Richardson, Texas, hosted by the Islamic Circle of North America (ICNA). The keynote speaker was Dr. Tariq Ramadan—an Islamic scholar and the grandson of Muslim Brotherhood founder Hassan al-Banna.

"Never mind how I managed to enter this highly guarded Islamic venue," Imani wrote, "but I witnessed their fund-raising methods and their goal to make America an Islamic land and eventually make Sharia law accepted by elected officials without a single bullet to be fired. . . . Tariq Ramadan encouraged Muslim attendees not to assimilate to American culture, but stealthily engage in political institutions, universities and run for political office. Then they will be in a position of power to drastically alter our way of life."

Why have Islamists like Tariq Ramadan turned to stealth techniques of soft jihad in their quest to conquer the West? Imani explains, "Soft Jihad is practiced where the sword of jihad is not advisable, where Muslims are not strong enough to unsheathe their sword, where if the true nature of Islam is exposed, the public would likely stamp them out."[37]

Why was Tariq Ramadan preaching jihad in Texas in 2020? Sixteen years earlier, in 2004, the George W. Bush administration had barred Tariq Ramadan from the U.S. by revoking his visa because of his support for terrorism. But in 2010, Secretary of State Hillary Clinton reinstated Ramadan's visa without explanation.[38]

Since 2017, five women have come forth accusing Tariq Ramadan of rape; in September 2024, a Swiss court convicted Ramadan of one rape charge and sentenced him to three years in prison, with two years suspended.[39]

AN EPIC JIHAD?

One of the most expensive and large-scale examples of soft jihad in America is the East Plano Islamic Center, or EPIC City. The 402-acre Muslim community, which is under construction about forty miles northeast of Dallas, will include a thousand-home planned community, a mosque, retail shops, daycare facilities, medical clinics, and a K-12 school. A separate development of rural properties called EPIC Ranches is also planned.

According to Sam Westrop of the Middle East Forum, "Records published by the government of Plano, TX, indicate the city has given $219,000 to the controversial East Plano Islamic Center (EPIC), despite ongoing law enforcement investigations." Governor Greg Abbott has ordered the Texas Rangers to investigate (in the governor's words) "the proposed EPIC compound for potentially violating criminal law."

The religious head of the EPIC mosque and planned community is Yasir Qadhi, a Muslim scholar and theologian. According to Westrop, Qadhi has "openly expressed hatred for Jews and advanced Holocaust denial ideas." He is on record as having "advocated the killing of homosexuals." After the October 7, 2023, slaughter and kidnapping of Israelis by Hamas terrorists, Qadhi praised the attacks "for putting 'horror in the hearts of the enemy.'"[40]

EPIC City has hired the high-profile Texas "Super Lawyer" Dan Cogdell, who won acquittals for defendants in the Enron case, the Texas Slave Ranch case, and the trial of embattled Texas attorney general Ken Paxton. Cogdell suggests that investigations of EPIC City are motivated by anti-Islamic bias, saying, "What is crazy to me is how far we haven't come since 9/11. The words 'mosque,' 'Islam,' 'Muslim' in the year of our Lord 2025 are still such a triggering event."[41]

But to anyone who has a clear understanding of Islamism, the EPIC City project *should* be a "triggering event." The United States was founded as a "melting pot," a land where many cultures, traditions, and religions could come together, maintaining their unique individuality while living in unity alongside other cultures, traditions, and religions. The deliberate mingling of cultures—not the creation of isolated, unassimilated enclaves—is the essence of the American experience.

The father of the Constitution, James Madison, warned in the *Federalist Papers* of the dangers of isolated factions that lead people to more often "vex and oppress each other, than to co-operate for their common good." He worried that a faction of people motivated by impulses that are "adverse to the rights of other citizens" might lead to oppression.[42] I can think of no impulse more "adverse to the rights of other citizens" than Islamism. The founding vision of America cannot be fulfilled by enclaves of extremist Islam, as represented by EPIC City.

Although EPIC leaders and planners moderated their stance after state officials began investigating, the true aims of EPIC City were evident in its initial advertisements. The EPIC City development group, Community Capital Partners, originally stated that it would "limit sales to only persons we believe will contribute to the overall makeup of our community and are legally eligible to invest and buy property in the United States."

The Fair Housing Act prohibits housing discrimination based on religion or race. The wording that EPIC City would "limit sales" to people of a certain "overall makeup" seems to suggest that EPIC City would be a Muslim-only community, violating the Fair Housing Act. That language has since been scrubbed from the EPIC City website.[43]

STEALTHY SHARIA

Yasir Qadhi, the East Plano Islamic Center resident scholar, now says that EPIC City "is open for all, and anybody who's interested is more than welcome to apply." But he adds, "Obviously, we understand that it's going to have a greater appeal to those of a certain background." So instead of saying that EPIC City will "limit sales" to certain people, he now says that EPIC City would only appeal to people "of a certain background."[44] Either way, the net result is almost certainly a huge Muslim-only enclave in the middle of Texas.

State and federal officials have expressed concern that EPIC City will be governed by Sharia law, based on the Quran, instead of the laws of the United States and Texas. Governor Greg Abbott has stated flatly, "Sharia law is not allowed in Texas." In response, Yasir Qadhi told the *Dallas Morning News* that the only laws the EPIC City will enforce will be federal and state laws.[45]

But is that the truth? Muslims, remember, are permitted to practice *taqiyya* (religious deception of one's enemies) in order to achieve victory for Allah. So, would EPIC City be governed by Sharia law or not?

In an online video, Qadhi gives us a significant clue about his real beliefs about Sharia law versus the laws of the state. In this video, he is teaching from Quran 4:34, which says that if husbands fear that their wives will be disobedient, they should "admonish them and banish them to beds apart, and scourge them."[46]

When Qadhi interprets this passage, he never mentions the fact that wife-beating is a felony (in Texas, for example, a convicted spouse abuser faces up to ten years in prison and a $10,000 fine).[47] Why doesn't Qadhi say that wife-beating is a crime? Could it be that the only law he recognizes is Sharia law?

Qadhi says that Quran 4:34 gives a husband three steps for dealing with a disobedient wife. Step A, he says, is for the man to advise or admonish his wife: "Allah says, 'Advise her.' *Fa'izuhunna*, right? Tell her that this marriage is not going to flourish this way."

Step B, Qadhi says, is for the man to leave his wife alone for a while: "Abandon her, leave her in her bed. You go to the living room and you leave her in the bedroom. You make her understand that things are getting serious."

And what is Step C? Yasir Qadhi doesn't explicitly say the words "beat her" or "scourge her," because he doesn't have to. Muslim men are familiar with Quran 4:34. So Yasir Qadhi refers to wife-beating euphemistically as "Option C" or "the third thing that is mentioned in the Quran." He explains, "My philosophy or my *fatwa* is that in the cultures that we live in, this is an option, A, B, or C. It's not *wajib* [obligatory]. If you have to get to C, my advice is jump over C and move to divorce. . . . In the society and the times and the cultures that we live in, resorting to Option C is going to break the marriage."

Again, Yasir Qadhi never says that wife-beating is against the law—only that it will "break the marriage." He recommends that husbands in Western societies bypass the wife-beating "option" and go straight to divorce.

Is wife-beating ever an acceptable option in Qadhi's mind? Yes! "In some cultures," he says, "Option C might have saved the marriage. But in . . . Western cultures in particular . . . Option C is going to completely break the marriage. It's not going to flourish."[48]

Yasir Qadhi doesn't recognize federal and state laws. The only law he recognizes is Sharia. So when he tells the *Dallas Morning News* that the only laws the EPIC City will enforce will be federal and state laws,[49] I suspect he is practicing *taqiyya*, the religious deception of his enemies.

An investigative report in *Front Page* online magazine says that there is every reason to believe that "EPIC is a Sharia-adherent organization whose plans for expansion envision a parallel society, an Islamic society. . . . Its promotional video, posted April 20, 2025, on Instagram, makes clear that its goal is to establish a self-governed Islamic community, which means a community under the rule of Islamic Law."[50]

There is an Arabian fable about a traveler riding his camel in the desert. He stops for the night, sets up his tent, ties his camel to a stake outside, and goes inside to sleep. But the camel pokes his nose under the tent flap, telling his master, "My nose is cold. May I put my nose inside the tent to warm it up?" The traveler agrees.

A little later, the camel complains that his head is cold—so the traveler lets the camel put his head in the tent. Later, the camel says his neck is cold. This goes on until the camel is completely inside the warm tent—and the traveler is forced to sleep on the cold desert sand.

This is a fitting metaphor of how soft jihad works—how it is already working in communities all across Western civilization. The Islamists hope to establish the precedent of a Sharia-governed community on American soil—that's the camel's nose under the tent flap. They hope that their conquest of our civilization will be so gradual that no one will notice—until it is too late.

ENCLAVES IN MINNESOTA, BEACHHEADS IN MICHIGAN

A growing number of Muslim enclaves around the country pose a difficult challenge to Western civilization. Minneapolis, Minnesota, is now home to thousands of refugees from the troubled African nation of Somalia. About 40 percent of all Somalis in the United States live in Minnesota, and many are concentrated in a Minneapolis neighborhood known as "Little Mogadishu." Named for the capital of Somalia, Little Mogadishu has been an important recruiting ground for the terrorist organization Al-Shabaab. Law enforcement officers who enter the neighborhood often encounter hostility from its people.[51]

Michigan is another Islamist beachhead in the United States. In January 2021, the city of Hamtramck, Michigan, elected a Muslim mayor and an all-Muslim city council. City council members have frequently expressed bigotry against Jews. In May 2024, the city council passed a resolution calling for boycotts and sanctions against Israel. According to *The Washington Post*, Hamtramck—whose population was 90 percent Polish Catholic in 1970—became the first majority-Muslim city in America in 2013. This change in demographics is due to an influx of Muslim immigrants from Yemen, Bangladesh, and Bosnia over the past decade.[52]

After the October 7, 2023, Hamas murder spree in Israel, Hamtramck's mayor, Yemen-born Amer Ghalib, sided with Hamas and declared that there could be no peace with Israel. President Donald Trump has nominated Mayor Ghalib as U.S. ambassador to Kuwait despite objections from the Anti-Defamation League, the American Jewish Committee, and Stop Antisemitism.[53]

Not far from Hamtramck is Dearborn, the hometown of the Ford Motor Company and its founder, Henry Ford. Dearborn is also home to the largest mosque in North America and one of the largest Muslim populations in the United States. Steven Stalinsky of the Middle East Media Research Institute (MEMRI) has dubbed Dearborn "America's Jihad Capital." MEMRI specializes in translating and posting videos online that show what Islamist clerics and politicians in America are saying to their audiences in Arabic, including their advocacy of jihad and terrorism.

Stalinsky reported on a rally at the Ford Performing Arts Center in Dearborn where, days after the October 7 Hamas attacks, Imam Imran Salha of the Islamic Center of Detroit told a pro-Hamas crowd that the fire in their hearts would burn the state of Israel "until its demise." A year earlier, in October 2022, the U.S. Department of Homeland Security had given Imam Salha's mosque a grant of $150,000.

One week after the Hamas attacks, Imam Usama Abdulghani addressed a crowd in front of Dearborn's Henry Ford Centennial Library. An American-born Islamic scholar trained in Iran, Abdulghani called the October 7 massacre "one of the days of God" and a "miracle come true," carried about by "honorable" attackers who defended "the entire nation of Muhammad the messenger."

One of the most well-known religious influencers in the world is Ahmad Musa Jibril of Dearborn, who advocates holy war to thousands of followers on Twitter and Telegram. On the day of the October 7 massacres, Jibril's account retweeted, "The hearts haven't been overjoyed like this in so long." He has also called upon Muslims to spread the term "jihad" in their mosques and on social media.[54]

Dearborn's mayor is Abdullah H. Hammoud, a Shia Muslim born to Lebanese-American parents. Hammoud has never condemned the October 7 massacres, but he has complained loudly of so-called Islamophobia whenever Islamists are criticized. In an op-ed for *The New York Times*, Hammoud accused Israel of committing "genocide" during the war in Gaza but has never criticized Hamas for starting that war.[55]

Muslims—including some who are clearly radical Islamists—have made great strides in the United States, winning election to high political offices. In addition to the many Muslim mayors and city council members around the United States, five Muslims have been elected to the U.S. House of Representatives. But Muslim politicians in the United States have not been nearly as successful as Muslim politicians in Great Britain.

THE BRITISH PARLIAMENT—OCCUPIED TERRITORY?

Muslims have a strong presence in all levels of government in Great Britain—as you can easily see by simply checking the Wikipedia entry "List of British Muslim Politicians."[56] Though Muslims make up only 6.5 percent of the British population,[57] some of Great Britain's largest cities are led by Muslim mayors, including London,[58] Birmingham,[59] Sheffield,[60] Luton,[61] and Oldham.[62] The city of Oxford was led by Lubna Arshad, the "first Muslim woman of intersectional background," from 2023 to 2024.[63]

I don't claim that all Muslims in British government are Islamists—but some clearly are. After the Hamas invasion of Israel that killed 1,200 people, Member of Parliament Sammy Wilson of East Antrim, Northern Ireland, addressed the House of Commons. He recounted how, during the Hamas invasion, "brutal terrorists attacked innocent individuals, innocent citizens, burnt, raped, murdered, and tortured [them], and took them hostage." As he talked, Muslim Members of Parliament smirked, laughed, and shouted at him until the Deputy Speaker called for order.[64]

After that disgraceful incident, Amjad Taha posted on X, "Your British Parliament isn't just compromised. It's crawling with Islamist settlers in suits, turning Westminster into a Hamas echo chamber. . . . This isn't Parliament. It's occupied territory."[65]

Radical Islamists are conquering territory by using our Western laws against us, especially our immigration and asylum laws. The Quran calls Muslims to the sacred duty of *hijrah* (migration) and urges them to spread Islam by moving out and occupying non-Muslim lands. As they settle in democratic nations, they use the democratic laws of those societies to gain power and undermine those same laws.

Many Islamists have openly declared their goal of using Western democracy to impose Islam on society. A video posted by the *Breaking Battlegrounds* podcast shows a Muslim imam telling his listeners, "One day you're going to be the president of the United States of America. [There is] no one who can stop you from becoming president. Dream big! Have a vision. . . . Change is coming to America. And what is Allah telling us? *Kuntum khayra ummatin.* 'You're the best of nations.' You're better than everybody else. That's what Allah is saying. Let's work towards that. Let's work towards a Muslim mayor. . . . Nominate people for the school board. . . . Nominate people for the local township."[66]

The imam goes on to say that it's important for Muslims to have babies, because babies grow up to be voters. "The demographics change," he said. "Muslims have the highest population average. The Pew Foundation did this research study . . . and they said that Muslim households average 3.4 children per family. The white American has one child per family. . . . These are not just babies being born in hospitals. These are voters."[67]

And it's true—the Pew Research Center does predict rapid growth for the Muslim population in Europe. In 2020, there were an estimated 50 million Muslims in Europe, about 6 percent of the continent's total population. It is projected to reach 14 percent by 2050.[68]

RAPE JIHAD

On January 3, 2025, tech billionaire Elon Musk tweeted on X.com that British prime minister Keir Starmer "was complicit in the RAPE OF BRITAIN when he was head of Crown Prosecution for 6 years. Starmer must go and he must face charges for his complicity in the worst mass crime in the history of Britain."[69]

Musk's tweet stirred up a storm of controversy across Great Britain. Musk was tweeting about a series of mass rapes of British girls by gangs of men, most of them from Pakistan or of Pakistani descent. These crimes took place over decades. Despite a few newspaper stories and a handful of prosecutions, most were covered up.

"Since Elon Musk fanned the flames afresh in January," wrote journalist Mary Harrington, "Starmer has faced a storm of criticism for refusing to grant a fresh inquiry, only commissioning Baroness Louise Casey to conduct an audit of existing reports."[70]

Many people assumed that the Louise Casey report would be a whitewash of the problem, but when the Casey audit was released, its findings were devastating. The report showed that a culture of denial had allowed Muslim men to rape thousands of British girls without consequences. These "rape gangs" or "grooming gangs" terrorized more than fifty British cities and towns. The authorities and the media covered up the crimes out of fear of being branded "racist."[71]

The girls ranged in age from teenagers down to children younger than ten. Many were gang-raped, sold as slaves, locked in cages, tortured, and overdosed with drugs. Some were murdered in ways too awful to describe. Authorities who were supposed to protect Britain's children pretended it simply wasn't happening.[72]

The cover-up of this "rape jihad" against British girls was enabled in large part by a cowardly media establishment. Journalist Julie Bindel recalled how, in 2006, she pitched a story to *The Guardian*, Britain's daily national newspaper, about a missing fourteen-year-old girl who was victimized by a rape gang in Blackpool. Her editor rejected the story—not because it wasn't well sourced and verified but out of cowardly fear. "We would be called racist if we publish this," the editor said.

Julie Bindel eventually managed to get the story published in the *Sunday Times Magazine*. After the piece appeared, Bindel received criticism from many of her colleagues and the public, calling her a "racist" for writing a story critical of Pakistani immigrants—even though every word was true.[73]

Another British journalist, Andrew Anthony of the *Observer*, wrote a book in which he confessed his guilt in covering up the truth about Muslim extremists who had immigrated to Great Britain. In *The Fallout: How a Guilty Liberal Lost His Innocence*, Anthony admitted that he would sometimes "turn a blind eye to cultural practices that were problematic or difficult to reconcile with a liberal outlook."

Going undercover, Anthony worked as a driver for a London cab company—a company that employed many Muslim immigrants—and was struck by how many Muslim drivers had nothing but "cold contempt" for British society but admired the Taliban terrorists and Iran's Ayatollah Khomeini. Anthony chose not to report these facts out of fear that it would be perceived as a racist attack on an immigrant minority group. Only later did he regret failing his journalistic duty to report the truth.[74]

ELIZABETH'S STORY

In the English town of Rotherham, an estimated 1,400 girls were victimized by Pakistani rape gangs over several decades. One of those girls has become known in news reports as "Elizabeth" (not her real name).

In 2005, when Elizabeth was fourteen, she was waiting at a bus stop when a woman struck up a conversation with her. The woman, who seemed pleasant and friendly, was, in fact, a white British woman who had converted to Islam, and she was "grooming" Elizabeth on behalf of a Pakistani rape gang. After gaining Elizabeth's trust, the woman delivered the girl to the gang, who took her to another city to be drugged and raped repeatedly for days.

Elizabeth's father (known as "Jack" in news reports) had no idea what had happened to his daughter, but the police ignored Jack's frantic pleas for help in finding her. Week after week, he suffered a father's worst nightmare, not knowing whether his daughter was alive or dead—or what torments she might be suffering.

Finally, after ten weeks, the rape gang set Elizabeth free. When Jack was reunited with her, he hardly recognized her—Elizabeth, physically and emotionally exhausted, weighed just seventy pounds.

In the days that followed, Elizabeth disappeared from home again and again while her father was at work. She would go missing for hours or days. The gangs knew where to find her.

Jack made hundreds of phone calls to the police, begging for help. He asked whether there were any other victims of these gangs, but the police lied and claimed that they had received no other reports. In fact, they had received hundreds.

Only once did a police officer tell Jack the truth. When Jack demanded to know why the police were doing nothing to protect the girls of Rotherham, the policeman angrily snapped, "You know why! If it comes out what the Pakistanis are doing, there will be riots. . . . I'm only going to tell you once. It's been going on for at least thirty years!"

Jack finally figured out where the Pakistani men lived, and the next time she went missing, he went to the apartment. Hearing Elizabeth inside, he called the police. The police arrived—but instead of rescuing the girl from the rape den, they handcuffed Jack and drove him home.

As soon as the police left, Jack rushed back to the apartment, kicking the door and demanding that the men release his daughter. Police again showed up, arrested Jack for disturbing the peace, and took him to the police station. The arresting officers told him not to return to the apartment where his daughter was being abused because he would be endangering her life—and the lives of other girls who were being victimized.

The story of Elizabeth's ordeal, her father's anguish, and the plight of hundreds of other young rape victims in Rotherham remained unreported for a decade. An official investigation of police misconduct in the rape-gang scandal resulted in no firings, no disciplinary actions, just five written warnings. Jack has since suffered a stroke, a heart attack, and post-traumatic stress because of the suffering he and his daughter endured.

A series of investigations of the Rotherham rape scandal finally resulted in dozens of trials of British Muslim rapists and their accomplices—and the trials are expected to continue for years. Tragically, thousands of girls had to be victimized before the scandal came to light.

SACRIFICED TO KEEP A SECRET

"If only the police had listened to us," Jack reflected. "I blame the police as equally as the perpetrators because they allowed it to happen. The families were all sacrificed to keep this secret all those years ago. It still makes me fume now. They could have stopped it then. On a number of occasions, police officers came to our house calling us bad parents. But we were not bad parents, we were working parents."

Elizabeth is now a young mother in her thirties and has written a book, *Snatched*, about her ordeal. She reveals that her father "blames himself every single day, saying he could not protect me." But Elizabeth blames the police, saying her father has been "absolutely destroyed" by their dereliction of duty.[75]

Although the rape-gang crisis in Great Britain has been exposed, it has not been solved. British officials continue to harbor a community of Muslim men who view non-Muslim women as trash, to be sexually used, abused, and discarded. The "politically correct" dogmas of the secular left still compel officials to ignore child rape, torture, and even murder *if* these crimes are committed by Muslims. These officials worry more about being called "racists" or "Islamophobes" than they care about the destruction of innocent young lives.

There are an estimated 1,500 mosques and at least thirty Sharia councils in the United Kingdom (according to a study commissioned by the British Parliament).[76] The Office for National Statistics reports that the most popular baby name in Great Britain is Muhammad.[77] The United Kingdom is surrendering its culture to radical Islam.

Islamists have invaded Great Britain and are forcing the powers-that-be in that country to submit to rape jihad. Leftists in the British government and the British media are collaborating in their own destruction—and the destruction of Britain's children. The occupation and subjugation of Western civilization is well underway in Great Britain.

The Islamists are pursuing a different strategy in America, but a strategy that is every bit as dangerous to our civilization: jihad by petrodollars.

3

THE QATARI CONNECTION

When, in 2018, Adel al-Jubeir, Saudi Arabia's Minister of State for Foreign Affairs, took questions at an event hosted by the Council on Foreign Relations, an American attorney stood and asked whether Saudi Arabia was working to resolve its "falling out" with the neighboring nation of Qatar.

"It's not a falling out," Al-Jubeir replied wryly. "It's just that we don't want to have anything to do with them." The room erupted in laughter. Then Al-Jubeir turned serious as he explained *why* the Saudis want nothing to do with Qatar.

"The Qataris," he said, "since the mid-nineties, have been sponsoring radicals. They have been inciting people. They have become a base for the leadership for the Muslim Brotherhood. And the Muslim Brotherhood, you have to keep in mind, is what begot us [the terror group] Takfir wal-Hijra, which begot us [the terror group] Al-Qaeda, which begot us [the terror group] Al-Nusra.

"The Qataris allow their senior religious clerics to go on television and justify suicide bombings. That's not acceptable. The Qataris harbor and shelter terrorists. That's not acceptable. And [Abd al-Rahim] Al-Nashiri, who was the head of Al-Qaeda in the Arabian Peninsula in 2001, entered Saudi Arabia on a Qatari passport. We captured Al-Qaeda types coming into Saudi Arabia with Qatari passports. The Qataris know this, the Americans know this, the world knows this. . . .

"The Qataris use their media platforms to spread hate. The Qataris send weapons to Al-Qaeda-affiliated militias in Libya. The Qatari emir was conniving with Gaddafi on how to overthrow Saudi Arabia. . . .

"There's a list of terror financiers that the US puts out, the UN puts out, and a number of them are living openly in Qatar, raising money and giving it to bad people. Is this acceptable? It shouldn't be. . . . People see a young country, young leadership. The Qataris buy fancy buildings, they have a nice airline and people think, 'Wow, these Qataris are really modern.'

"But we have to deal with the dark side, that I just explained. And so that's why we said, 'Until and unless you change, we're not going to deal with you.' . . . We have no hostility towards Qatar. We just vehemently oppose their behavior, which is very dangerous."[78]

And yet everything Adel al-Jubeir said only scratches the surface of Qatar's subversive influence in the world. Though Qatar pretends to be a friend to America and the West, it is in fact an oil-rich Islamist nation that is cleverly waging jihad against us, using petrodollars as a weapon.

Our opinion leaders in the media don't get it. Our academic leaders don't get it. Even our political leaders in Washington, D.C., don't get it. This astonishing level of ignorance among our leaders threatens the future of our civilization.

THE QATARI HORSE

The Middle Eastern nation of Qatar is geographically smaller than the state of Connecticut. Demographically, Qatar has a citizen population of only 300,000 people (an additional 2.3 million people live in Qatar, most of them migrant workers). Qatar is a hotbed of Islamic radicalism, housing the headquarters of the Muslim Brotherhood. This tiny nation is the chief sponsor of Hamas terrorists. Qatar is also a longtime safe haven for the Taliban, and a diplomatic partner of Iran.

Yet tiny Qatar is having a huge—and largely hidden—impact on American education, media, commerce, and politics. What is the reason for Qatar's disproportionate influence on America? Money—lots and lots of money. Qatar sits on one of the largest natural gas and oil reserves in the world. And Qatar is using its petrodollars to call the shots all across the Western world, and especially in the United States.

According to a troubling report by Frannie Block and Jay Solomon of The Free Press, several key members of the Trump administration have close ties to Qatar. Attorney General Pam Bondi and White House Chief of Staff Susie Wiles have both worked for lobbying firms that represented Qatar. FBI Director Kash Patel was a paid consultant to Qatar. White House senior advisor Steve Witkoff benefited in 2023 when Qatar's sovereign wealth fund purchased his interest in New York's Park Lane Hotel for $623 million.

The most obvious symbol of Qatar's efforts to influence American foreign policy is the gift of a $400-million Boeing 747-8 jetliner to President Trump—a luxury aircraft that has been called "the palace in the sky." The White House directed the Air Force to convert the plane into a new Air Force One.

Despite a chorus of criticism from politicians and the press, President Trump accepted the Qatari jet, declaring that only "a stupid person" would refuse the gift of "a free, very expensive airplane."[79] One wonders: Is Mr. Trump familiar with story of the Trojan Horse?

The Trojan Horse is an episode in Virgil's *Aeneid*. After besieging Troy for ten years, the Greeks, led by Odysseus, built a giant wooden horse and hid soldiers inside. The Trojans, believing the horse was a gift, pulled it inside the city gates. At night, Odysseus and his men emerged from the horse and opened the gates, allowing the Greek army to enter and conquer Troy.

The "palace in the sky" and other Qatari "gifts" are Trojan horses. I'm not suggesting that President Trump or anyone else in his administration has done anything improper; nor am I saying that these contacts with Qatar are a problem for Republicans alone. In fact, Qatar is using its considerable wealth to court Democrats as well as Republicans. Members of both parties have taken all-expense-paid junkets to meet with the Qatar Foundation, which spends millions annually to influence American universities and politicians.

Members of Congress who have met with the Qatar Foundation in Doha include Eric Swalwell (D-California), Ruben Gallego (D-Arizona), Jim Himes (D-Connecticut), Seth Moulton (D-Massachusetts), Sara Jacobs (D-California), Lou Correa (D-California), and Lisa McClain (R-Michigan). *Business Insider* has posted photos to social media showing Swalwell and Gallego jubilantly riding camels shirtless in the Qatari desert.[80]

Do these political leaders know that the Qatar Foundation has links to Hamas and the Muslim Brotherhood? A pro-Israel think tank, the Lawfare Project, states that the Qatar Foundation is infiltrating American schools and turning "school teachers into de facto agents of the Qatari government, conveying its political (and antisemitic) views to students and the general population without any acknowledgment of the origins of these views."[81]

Qatari influence poses a uniquely dangerous threat to Western civilization. The entire nation of Qatar has a citizen population the size of a modest American city. Yet, through a strategic use of oil wealth, subterfuge, and propaganda, Qatar has become a puppet master in American education, media, and politics.

Few people understand the danger we face. As in the story of the Trojan Horse, our political and opinion leaders have accepted the wooden horse the Qataris have offered us as a "free gift" and have pulled it inside our gates. It's just a matter of time before the "Qatari Horse" destroys us.

QATARI SPORTSWASHING

The term "sportswashing" is a new term to me, and refers to the practice of a government using sports to improve a reputation that has been tarnished by scandals or bad publicity. A government will host sports events or purchase a sports team in order to build up a positive image among sports fans. Sportswashing is considered a form of "reputation laundering."

Qatar has hosted a number of high-profile sports events that many commentators view as sportswashing, including the 2020 FIFA Club World Cups and the 2022 FIFA World Cup. (FIFA is the Fédération Internationale de Football Association, the governing body of world soccer.) Qatar also acquired the Paris Saint-Germain Football Club, which boasts more soccer trophies than any other club in France.

Qatar spent about $6.5 billion to construct and renovate the eight soccer stadiums for the 2022 FIFA World Cup, its total investment in the World Cup estimated at about $220 billion. Most of that money was spent on improving infrastructure around the Qatari soccer facilities—hospitality, transportation, telecommunications, and more.[82]

The attempt to sportswash Qatar's image by hosting the first World Cup in the Middle East backfired when journalists and human-rights activists looked into the treatment of the migrant workers who constructed the soccer stadiums. Workers were forced to live in cramped, unclean housing, were lied to about working conditions and pay, were assessed hidden fees, and sometimes went for months without a paycheck. When they complained, they were threatened, their passports confiscated, and were not allowed to quit or leave the country.[83] As a result, some human-rights groups claim Qatar used "slave labor" to build its stadiums.[84]

The Journal of Democracy compares sportswashing to a "character reference." If a person with a good reputation shares a testimonial about you, he lends credibility to your cause—whether you deserve credibility or not. In 2019, Qatar hosted British soccer star David Beckham at Qatar's World Cup facilities. Exactly as his hosts intended, Beckham praised Qatar's "great" stadiums and "safe" hotels, which meant that people who might otherwise have hesitated to attend the World Cup in a little-known Middle Eastern country were reassured by Beckham's words.[85]

Ultimately, Qatar's attempt to rebrand itself—at a cost of hundreds of billions of dollars—fell flat, and before the 2022 FIFA World Cup in Qatar, British adults had a 67 percent unfavorable view of Qatar. After the World Cup, that unfavorable view had increased to 72 percent.[86]

As social psychology researcher Yair Galily observed, "Qatar has utilized soft power to amplify its global influence through cultural diplomacy, media, and sports. Al Jazeera and events like the 2022 FIFA World Cup have positioned Qatar as a modern, forward-thinking state despite controversies over labor rights, LGBTQ+ policies, and alleged ties to extremist groups. These contradictions challenge its soft power credibility."[87]

JIHAD THROUGH EDUCATION

In recent years, many American university campuses have been rocked by pro-Hamas protests, bullying, and violence, with activists engaged in standoffs with university personnel and police. These actions were led by such groups as Students for Justice in Palestine, American Muslims for Palestine, and the Islamic Association for Palestine—all organizations spawned by, or aligned with, the radical Muslim Brotherhood.

Islamist activists have bullied students, shouted chants and threats, and blocked hallways to prevent students from attending classes. After the October 7, 2023, Hamas terror rampage in southern Israel, activists ripped down posters of hostages held by Hamas, and physically attacked those students who put up posters.[88]

How did Islamism come to be such a dominant force in American academia? How have so many American universities been captured by this virulent anti-American, anti-Jewish, anti-Christian ideology? The answer: American universities have been seduced by truckloads of foreign cash, most of it from Qatar.

Take, for example, the corruption of Georgetown University, the once-respected institution founded by a Jesuit bishop in 1789. The Institute for the Study of Global Antisemitism and Policy (ISGAP) reports that Georgetown and other universities have received billions of dollars in "illicit funding" from foreign entities linked to terrorism and Islamism. ISGAP's research shows that the Muslim Brotherhood has, in fact, conducted a fifty-year campaign at Georgetown to turn this elite institution into a hotbed of Islamist extremism.[89] ISGAP reports that Qatari money has had a profound impact at Georgetown:

> Over the past fifty years, Georgetown University has transformed from a prestigious academic institution rooted in Jesuit traditions into a pivotal nexus where radical ideologies, academic inquiry, and geopolitical influence converge. This transformation is largely attributable to decades of substantial foreign funding from Middle Eastern countries—including Oman, Saudi Arabia, Kuwait, Egypt, Jordan, and Qatar, the largest funder of them all—which have not only redefined Georgetown's academic and cultural identity but also steered its intellectual discourse toward a distinctive pro-Islamist and anti-Israel orientation.[90]

After the October 7 Hamas massacre of 1,200 Israelis, Bruce Hoffman—a Georgetown professor who focuses on terrorism and insurgency studies—posted on X.com, "Of course Hamas acquired this arsenal using the largesse bestowed on it from Iran as well as Qatar." After Hoffman posted the comment, he was contacted by a former Defense Department official with a message from the Pentagon: The Qataris were unhappy with his post on X, and the Pentagon wanted him to stop tweeting. Hoffman's remarks, they said, might "endanger" the U.S. Al Udeid Air Base in Qatar.

The American base in Qatar may have given the U.S. a strategic foothold in the Middle East—but it also gave Qatar leverage over the Pentagon. A Qatari official could pick up the phone, express his country's displeasure—and suppress the free speech of a Georgetown professor. Every American should find this incident chilling.[91]

In October 2024, after the Israeli Defense Force cornered and killed Yahya Sinwar, the mastermind of the October 7 Hamas attacks, Sheikha Moza bint Nasser—the mother of Qatar's Emir—posted a message of praise for the slain terrorist leader on X.com. She wrote, "The name Yahya means the one who lives. They thought him dead but he lives. Like his namesake, Yahya bin Zakariya, he will live on and they [the Israelis] will be gone."[92]

Six months after Sheikha Moza posted those pro-terrorist sentiments, Georgetown University honored her with the Georgetown University President's Medal, recognizing, among other things, her service in "the promotion of peace and social justice." In that ceremony, Georgetown subserviently renewed its agreement of cooperation with Qatar for another ten years.[93]

It is a sad spectacle to see a university founded on Christian principles now reduced to groveling and spouting lies in exchange for oil-soaked, bloodstained Qatari cash.

SUBVERSION AND INDOCTRINATION OF YOUNG MINDS

Georgetown is, however, just one among many American universities that has been subverted by Qatari petrodollars. "Foreign countries such as China and Qatar have poured $29 billion into campuses over the past few years," The Free Press reported in early 2025, adding that this figure "is more than double the total for the preceding four years, and accounts for half of the estimated $57.97 billion in foreign funding since 1986, when the federal government began tracking the data."

The Free Press cited a study by the Network Contagion Research Institute (NCRI)—an organization dedicated to identifying ideologically motivated threats from hate groups, political ideologies, propaganda, and disinformation. The NCRI study found that the tiny nation of Qatar is "the largest source of foreign donations to U.S. universities since reporting began in 1986, with $6.3 billion coming from the gas-rich Gulf state. . . . Qatari donations have ramped up significantly over the last four years. Nearly a third of donations from Qatar—over $2 billion—were given between 2021 and 2024."

ISGAP has reported an enormous flow of money from Qatari foundations to leading American universities, including Cornell, Carnegie Mellon, Georgetown, Northwestern, Texas A&M, Virginia

Commonwealth, and many more. The Qatari organizations, which include the Qatar Foundation and Qatar National Research Fund, serve as proxies to hide the direct involvement of the Qatari government in a massive attempt to influence what is taught in American universities.[94]

Joel Finkelstein, co-founder of the Network Contagion Research Institute, observed, "This isn't just a financial issue—it's a national security crisis. Hostile powers are buying influence on American campuses at an industrial scale."[95]

Why do foreign nations invest billions of dollars in American universities? Are they motivated by sheer altruism—a desire to shower benefits on Western academia out of the goodness of their hearts? Or do they expect something in return? Do they want power? Control? The ability to indoctrinate young Western minds? Of this we can be sure: Foreign nations expect something in return for their money—and they're getting it.

Section 117 of the Higher Education Act requires American colleges and universities to report foreign donations exceeding $250,000, including research contracts. But, according to the American Enterprise Institute, many academic institutions simply flout the law and refuse to disclose foreign donations.[96]

The Qatari strategy of jihad through education doesn't, of course, stop with university students. Qatar is even targeting American public school children in grades K through 12. The Qatar Foundation International (QFI) has donated millions of dollars to fund Arabic language and culture programs in public schools from Connecticut to California. QFI has also funded the salaries for Arabic teachers in the Minneapolis Public School District—with the requirement that those teachers must undergo QFI's training.[97]

Qatar has established a mega-campus called Education City, located in Al Rayyan Municipality in the Doha metropolitan area of Qatar, and has invited a number of leading American universities to set up schools at Education City. Georgetown has a school of foreign service in Education City, Cornell has a medical school there, Texas A&M an engineering school, and Northwestern a journalism school.

Universities that participate in the Education City environment have to submit to Qatar's speech restrictions, however. It's against the law in Qatar to criticize the government or the royal family, or to question Islam, so students on Education City campuses, whether American or from other cultures, learn to submit to Qatari restrictions on speech and freedom.

Qatar's oppressive influence can even extend from Education City to the American homeland. On one occasion, Georgetown students were invited to an extravagant dinner at the Qatari embassy in Washington. The speaker was Majed al-Ansari, an official with the Qatar Ministry of Affairs. When a student asked about human-rights abuses in Qatar, Al-Ansari reprimanded the student for "colonialist thinking."[98] Islamists like Al-Ansari have become skilled at using the language and tactics of the secular left to control the conversation.

A HOME FOR THE MUSLIM BROTHERHOOD

When, in August 2004, a Maryland police officer spotted a woman in traditional Islamic attire taking a video of the structural supports of the Chesapeake Bay Bridge, he detained the woman, which led to the FBI searching her house in Annandale, Virginia. The house contained a secret basement with a trove of jihadist documents.

One of those documents, titled *An Explanatory Memorandum: On the General Strategic Goal for the Group*, was written by senior Hamas leader Mohammed Akram, and the "Group" it refers to was the Muslim Brotherhood. The document had been produced in 1987 for the Muslim Brotherhood's Shura Council and Organizational Conference, and contained this ominous mission statement:

> The process of settlement [of Islamists in Western countries] is a "Civilization-Jihadist Process" with all the word means. The *Ikhwan* [the Arab name for the Brotherhood] must understand that their work in America is a kind of grand jihad in eliminating and destroying the Western civilization from within and "sabotaging" its miserable house by their

> hands and the hands of the believers so that it is eliminated and [Allah's] religion is made victorious over all other religions.[99]

The document lays out a strategy of infiltrating and destroying Western civilization from within—a strategy that the Muslim Brotherhood is still pursuing today.

The Muslim Brotherhood is a transnational Islamist organization founded in 1928 by an Egyptian Islamic elementary-school teacher by the name of Hassan al-Banna, its stated goal being to establish a global caliphate ruled by Sharia law. For many years, the Brotherhood used political violence—including terrorism and assassination—to achieve its goals.

Though the Muslim Brotherhood has spawned or inspired many brutal terrorist groups, it now claims to be a peaceful, democratic organization. Yet this supposedly "peaceful" group continues to use a flag featuring two crossed swords and the Arabic phrase *Wa-aiidu*, "Prepare!"—a command taken from Quran 8:60, a call to wage war against the unbelievers.

Today, the Muslim Brotherhood is one of the most influential Islamist movements in history, with branches across the Middle East and in many parts of the world, including America and Europe. The motto of the Muslim Brotherhood is, "Allah is our objective. The Prophet is our leader. Quran is our law. Jihad is our way. Dying in the way of Allah is our highest hope."[100]

In the 1950s and 1960s, many Muslim Brotherhood members left Egypt and other Middle Eastern nations, fleeing government crackdowns. Many members settled in Qatar, and the oil-rich state of Qatar has since played a major role in the trajectory of the Brotherhood. Qatar has fostered a welcoming environment for the Brotherhood's brand of radical Islamism and has provided a platform—the Al Jazeera media megaphone—to amplify its message to the world.

In the 1950s and 1960s, Qatar was an emerging oil producer and still a British protectorate (it would become an independent state in 1971). Lacking a class of educated and skilled professionals,

Qatar welcomed the exiled Muslim Brotherhood members, who filled key vacancies in Qatar's professional sector and schools. Whereas the Brotherhood had been an underground movement in Egypt, its members could operate openly in Qatar.

What is the Muslim Brotherhood's connection to the terror group Hamas? The word Hamas is an acronym in Arabic for *Ḥarakat al-Muqāwamah al-ʾIslāmiyyah* ("The Islamic Resistance Movement"), which emerged from the Palestinian intifada ("uprising") in 1987 and was founded by Sheikh Ahmed Yassin as an offshoot of a charity run by the Brotherhood. The stated goal of Hamas: to eliminate Israel and install an Islamic state of Palestine.

Qatar has hosted the political bureau of Hamas for more than two decades, with the Qataris having donated billions of dollars to Hamas. While the impoverished people of Gaza are used by Hamas as cannon fodder and human shields, the top officials of Hamas's political wing enjoy the opulent splendor of Qatari luxury hotels. The top three leaders of Hamas have a combined net worth of $11 billion.[101]

AL JAZEERA—QATAR'S POWERFUL PROPAGANDA MACHINE

The 1996 launch of the state-funded satellite network Al Jazeera provided a global platform for Islamist voices, including the voice of the Muslim Brotherhood. Yusuf al-Qaradawi, an Egyptian cleric who was long considered the Brotherhood's chief spiritual leader, became a celebrity on Al Jazeera, hosting a talk show, *Sharia and Life*, until his death in 2022. One of the topics he discussed was why suicide bombings are justified by the Quran.[102]

Al Jazeera's coverage of regional affairs lent credibility and visibility to the Muslim Brotherhood and its allies, and Qatar's eagerness to amplify radical voices on the platform has made the network the epicenter of radical political Islam. Al Jazeera is, however, a weapon of mass persuasion that Qatar uses to advance its "soft jihad" strategy.

On January 24, 2025, Al Jazeera aired a special episode of a news show called *What Is Hidden Is Greater*. It included exclusive interviews and camera footage supplied by Hamas, and it told a false version of the October 7 invasion of Israel. According to the report, Hamas terrorists only targeted Israeli soldiers and were careful not to harm children or other civilians. The attack, the report added, was an unqualified victory for Hamas. The host, Palestinian journalist Tamer Almisshal, ended with praise for Hamas's historic assault against Israel.[103]

While Al Jazeera claims to provide balanced journalism, its messaging leans heavily toward Islamism and Hamas. On one occasion, an Al Jazeera reporter was interviewing a wounded man in Gaza, and seemed to want the man to blame Israel for his injuries. Instead, the man criticized Hamas for using civilians as human shields—so the reporter simply ended the interview and walked away.[104]

AL JAZEERA AND AMERICAN MEDIA

Al Jazeera, the state-run news channel of Qatar, has influenced American media by means of a project called AJ+, which combines news and social media to sway public opinion. AJ+ operates three accounts on X.com: @ajplus, @ajplusarabi, and @ajplusfrancais. These accounts engage with other accounts on X, many of which have been identified as fake accounts or "bots." These discussions are then seen by journalists, who repeat the Qatari propaganda narratives.

The style guide used by Al Jazeera instructs reporters to use language in a way that controls the thinking of its readers and viewers. For example, Al Jazeera journalists are required to describe any Palestinian who dies in combat—whether a civilian or a terrorist—as a "martyr," and all Israeli-controlled land—including the land within the 1949 borders recognized by the UN—is called "the occupation."[105]

As The Free Press reported in 2025, "Al Jazeera is the ultimate soft-power tool. According to documents shared by the Israeli military last fall, at least six Al Jazeera journalists were active members of Hamas and Palestinian Islamic Jihad."[106]

Al Jazeera is thus a powerful propaganda weapon funded and controlled by tiny, oil-rich Qatar. From lavishing expensive gifts on Western politicians to hosting global sporting events, from indoctrinating Western students to shaping Western public opinion, the Qatari connection is a web of subversive relationships. Though Qatar is tiny and sparsely populated, its enormous oil and gas reserves have given the Qatari ruling family the global influence of a superpower. And Qatar unapologetically supports such dangerous Islamist networks as Hamas and the Muslim Brotherhood.

Now more than ever, Westerners—and especially Western leaders—should beware of Qataris bearing gifts.

4

A SHORT HISTORY OF JIHAD

In early June 2025, central Los Angeles was flooded with protesters who burned cars and clashed with police. For hours, police were pinned down under a freeway overpass as protesters hurled chunks of cement, fireworks, and other deadly objects at them.[107] It looked like the end of civilization.

The unrest erupted in response to attempts by U.S. Immigration and Customs Enforcement (ICE) to serve warrants and detain illegal immigrants. A number of far-left groups joined the protests, including a group called Unity of Fields, formerly known as Palestine Action U.S., a militantly anti-American, anti-Israeli, pro-Hamas organization.

Unity of Fields activists called for Los Angeles to be burned and celebrated the wounding of police officers, urging people to rise up in an intifada against ICE and the police. Unity of Fields had thus brought jihad to the streets of Los Angeles.

During the protests, a man emerged from the crowd with a Hamas scarf encircling his arm and a Popular Front for the Liberation of Palestine headband on his brow, waving a Mexican flag. He approached a Waymo Jaguar I-Pace self-driving car, one of many driverless cars summoned to the scene by protestors. Using a chemical accelerant, the protestor set the car ablaze, causing the car's lithium-ion battery to burn at temperatures above 1,800 degrees F, vaporizing much of the car and releasing clouds of toxic smoke.[108]

Utilizing the Telegram-encrypted messaging service, Unity of Fields activists coordinated the violent actions of 10,000 people they called "the Hamas Marxist army." They told reporters, "L.A. Intifada is one part of the international revolutionary sequence that was opened up by the *Toufan Al-Aqsa*"—that is, "Operation Al-Aqsa Flood," the name Hamas gave to its October 7 surprise attack against Israel.[109]

The Los Angeles riots were carefully orchestrated and well funded. An unknown wealthy benefactor shipped truckloads of so-called bionic shields to the protesters. These shields are transparent visors that protect the wearer from splashed chemicals or chunks of debris. News crews captured video of people distributing these shields to protesters. The shields, valued at about $60 each, were still in their factory packaging. News crews also spotted protesters putting on shields and gas masks.[110]

DEDICATED TO VIOLENCE AND DESTRUCTION

Why would Unity of Fields—a radical jihadist organization—join forces with anti-ICE protesters? Why would Palestinian jihadists care if ICE rounds up illegal immigrants from Mexico, El Salvador, or Venezuela? How were street battles in Los Angeles supposed to help jihadists in Gaza, on the other side of the world?

Here, again, we see the Red-Green Omnicause in action.

Unity of Fields was founded in 2023 and held its first "militant propaganda" events immediately after the October 7 Hamas attacks. The group has openly dedicated itself to "direct action"—that is, to violence and destruction of property. Unity of Fields has vandalized the office of New York congressman Adriano Espaillat and the Washington, D.C., office of the American Israel Public Affairs Committee, and called for protesters to set police officers on fire at the University of Washington—to name just a few of its "direct actions."[111]

The name "Unity of Fields" refers to the strategy of waging jihad through a "unity of the battlefields"—in Arabic, *Wahdat al-Sahat*—and this means coordinating warfare across multiple battlefronts at the same time. To the extremists of Unity of Fields, the Los Angeles battlefield is simply an extension of the Gaza battlefield. This multiple-battlefield strategy puts extra pressure and strain on the enemy—and the enemy is Western civilization.[112]

For more than fourteen centuries, Islamists have sought to impose their political religion on the world—by persuasion, if possible; by force, if necessary, but always by jihad (by struggle). Though the Arabic word *jihad* can refer to an inward, spiritual struggle against temptation and sin, radical Islamists almost exclusively speak of jihad as a struggle against the enemies of Islam. To understand the forces that oppose us, let's take a brief tour of the history of jihad.

THE ORIGIN OF JIHAD

According to Muslim tradition, Muhammad—forty years old at the time—received a revelation from the angel Gabriel while meditating in a cave on Mount Hira, near Mecca, in AD 610. This is said to be the founding of Islam.

After his experience in the cave, Muhammad began preaching in Mecca, and his followers quickly grew in number. At first, Islam seemed to be a peaceful religion, and his message didn't stir up any opposition from Muhammad's tribesmen, the Quraysh. In fact, the Quraysh had no interest in his new religion. But when Muhammad began denouncing the Quraysh for their unbelief, he stirred up a hornet's nest of opposition.

The early Muslims, being a minority in Mecca, suffered severe persecution (including torture and death) from the Quraysh, the dominant tribe. During this time of persecution in Mecca, the Muslims developed a concept of jihad as armed resistance against unbelievers.

In 622, when Muhammad learned that the Quraysh were plotting to kill him, he gathered his few hundred followers and migrated from Mecca to Medina, the *Hijra* (migration) to Medina marking the beginning of the Islamic calendar. After Muhammad's death in 632, Islam continued to spread through military conquest.

When Muhammad founded the Muslim faith, he named it *Islam*, which means "submission," and taught that every individual human being and every nation on Earth must submit to Allah and the teachings of Islam. Since its founding, radical Islam has never lost sight of the goal of a one-world government under the absolute rule of an Islamic *caliph* (ruler).

THE THREE GREAT JIHADS

Radical Muslims pursue their goal of world conquest though jihad, and there have been three major waves of jihad in history, each intended to expand the territory of Islam.

The First Jihad was the Age of the Caliphs, from AD 622 through 750. Thus was a jihad of the sword, of military conquest, and included the expansion of Islamic rule under Muhammad (622–632), under the Rashidun Caliphate (632–661), and under the Umayyad Caliphate (661–750). By the end of this era, Islam had conquered land as far west as Spain, Portugal, and Morocco—and as far east as Pakistan and India.

In 732, Abdul Rahman Al Ghafiqi led an army of Umayyad horse soldiers from Muslim-ruled Spain on an expedition deep into France, his goal to conquer France for Allah. At the hamlet of Moussais, near the city of Tours, the Muslim army fought the French infantry of Charles Martel, prince of the Franks. In what is now known as the Battle of Tours, Martel's army defeated the Muslim invaders and so halted the First Jihad.

The Second Jihad was the rise, expansion, and decline of the Ottoman Empire, from approximately 1299 to 1924. This, too, was a jihad of military conquest. At its height, the Ottoman Empire—founded by the Turkish tribal leader Osman I around 1299—dominated north Africa, southeastern Europe, and western Asia. In 1302, Osman and his followers defeated the Byzantine army at the Battle of Bapheus—and the Ottoman Empire began its ascent. In 1453, the Ottomans conquered Constantinople (now Istanbul) and consigned the Byzantine Empire to history.

Christian armies stopped the Ottoman forces outside of Vienna—twice. The first time was during the Siege of Vienna in 1529 when the Ottoman sultan, Suleiman the Magnificent, laid siege to Vienna with a force of more than 100,000 men. In a battle lasting just over two weeks, the outnumbered Christian defenders, led by Count Niklas of Salm, fought off the Muslim army with just 21,000 soldiers.

A century and a half later, the Ottoman invaders again besieged Vienna, the Battle of Vienna fought at nearby Kahlenberg Mountain on September 12, 1683. This time round, the Ottomans were led by Grand Vizier Merzifonlu Kara Mustafa Pasha, whose army numbered 170,000 men. The Christian defenders of Vienna consisted of the army of the Holy Roman Empire and the army of Poland, both of which were commanded by King John III Sobieski of Poland. Sobieski led a charge of 18,000 horsemen—the largest cavalry charge in history—which broke the battle lines of the Ottomans, forcing them to retreat.

The Battle of Vienna was a turning point. From then on, the Ottomans could no longer sustain their expensive conquests, and the Empire gradually declined in both power and influence. The Ottoman decline culminated in a humiliating defeat in World War I and Turkey's abolishment of the Ottoman Caliphate in 1924.

That's a brief history of the First and Second Jihads. But what about the Third Jihad? Though few Westerners realize it, the Third Jihad is happening *now*.

EXPLOITING OUR FREEDOMS TO DESTROY OUR FREEDOMS

Though Islamists have not abandoned the sword, the Third Jihad is primarily a struggle of stealth and infiltration. This does not mean that all Muslims migrating to Europe and North America are engaging in jihad—far from it. Most Muslims who come to the West are looking to improve their lives and want to peacefully assimilate into Western society.

At the same time, there are millions of determined Islamists moving into our midst, establishing beachheads in Western civilization with a goal of one day establishing a global caliphate. It can be difficult to distinguish mainstream Muslims on one hand from radical Islamists on the other. Let's define our terms:

Islamism is a political belief system that seeks to force both the government and surrounding society to submit to totalitarian Islamic rule. An *Islamist* is an Islamic fundamentalist who fervently believes that the religion of Islam is not merely a personal choice but should control every aspect of society and government, whether people willingly accept Islam or not. Islamists believe in using our democratic freedoms to undermine democracy and freedom, and to eventually install an Islamist theocracy.

We are now engulfed in a third wave of Islamic jihad—and Islam is winning. During previous waves of jihad, Christians in Europe valiantly defended their gates against invasion. Today, leftists and Progressives use their political and cultural clout to throw open the gates of their nations, collaborating with the jihadists in ways that can only be described as cultural suicide.

Is it too late? Have we passed the tipping point? Are the jihadists destined to win?

THE ORIGINS OF THE THIRD JIHAD

The origins of the Third Jihad can be traced to Egyptian schoolteacher Hassan al-Banna. Born in 1906, Al-Banna was deeply affected by the decline of the Ottoman Caliphate and the presence of European colonial power in Egypt, convinced that a return to ancient Islamic principles was essential for the revival of the Muslim world. In 1928, he gathered six like-minded men and founded what would become the Muslim Brotherhood, with a goal of restoring Islamic religious purity and removing Western influence from the Muslim world.

The Muslim Brotherhood grew rapidly under Hassan al-Banna's leadership. Even after Al-Banna was assassinated in 1949, the movement he founded continued to grow in numbers and influence.

In 1952, the Muslim Brotherhood supported a military coup that overthrew the Egyptian monarchy—but were disappointed when the victorious military junta refused to share power with the Brotherhood. In October 1954, the Brotherhood thus attempted to assassinate Colonel Gamal Abdel Nasser, head of the ruling military junta—but Nasser survived, and the Egyptian government hunted down and executed many Brotherhood members, many others escaping to neighboring countries, especially Qatar.

In the 1970s, the Muslim Brotherhood finally rebranded itself as a "humanitarian" organization, attracting donations from Westerners fooled by this disguise. The Brotherhood's charitable work is designed to obscure its real aims, which is to undermine Western society and advocate for Sharia law.

In 2001, the Muslim Brotherhood's London publication, *Risalat al-Ikhwan* ("Epistles of the Brethren of Purity") featured the slogan "Our Mission: World Domination." After the 9/11 terrorist attacks, the editors removed this slogan from the publication—but world domination is still the mission of the Muslim Brotherhood.[113]

In 2004, Muhammad Mahdi Othman Akef, the Supreme Guide of the Muslim Brotherhood from 2004 to 2010, declared, "I have complete faith that Islam will invade Europe and America, because Islam has logic and a mission."[114]

Akef's successor, Mohammed Badi (now serving multiple life sentences for his involvement in violent crimes in Egypt[115]), said in 2010 that the Muslim Brotherhood movement "knows nothing but the language of force, so [the Muslims] must meet iron with iron. . . . The improvement and change that the [Muslim] nation seeks can only be attained through jihad and sacrifice and by raising a jihadi generation that pursues death just as the enemies pursue life."[116]

No one should be fooled by the Muslim Brotherhood's attempt to recast itself as a "peaceful" and "humanitarian" organization. Nothing has changed but the Brotherhood's approach to public relations.

Its goal remains the same: world domination in the name of Islam.

Its method remains the same: jihad by armed struggle and by deception.

Its language remains the same: the language of force.

THE SPREADING CONTAGION OF JIHAD

Though the main body of the Muslim Brotherhood tries to present itself as peaceful, it is the tree that has yielded the poisonous fruit of armed jihad and terrorism. Perhaps the most infamous offshoot of the Muslim Brotherhood is Hamas (the Islamic Resistance Movement), formed in 1987 during the first Palestinian intifada (uprising). It began as the official Palestinian branch of the Muslim Brotherhood and was designated as a foreign terrorist organization by the U.S. Department of State in 1997.

Al-Qaeda was directly inspired by the Muslim Brotherhood's ideology, the founders of Al-Qaeda being students of early Muslim Brotherhood leaders such as Sayyid Qutb, who advocated for violent jihad to establish governments that are ruled by Sharia law. In fact, the founders of the Islamic State (ISIS)—a radical Islamist terrorist group that splintered from Al-Qaeda—were directly inspired by the writings of Muslim Brotherhood leaders Hassan al-Banna and Sayyid Qutb. In turn, both HASM (Harakat Sawa'id Misr, the Arms of Egypt Movement) and Liwa al-Thawra (the Revolution Brigade) are offshoots of the Egyptian Muslim Brotherhood. They have committed bombings and assassinations of senior Egyptian officials and are designated as terrorist organizations by several countries, including the United States and the United Kingdom.

And these are just a few of the violent jihadist organizations either spawned or inspired by the Muslim Brotherhood and its teachings. The ideological descendants of Al-Banna and the Muslim Brotherhood now seek to restructure *all* governments and *all* societies in conformance to Islamic law. They do not want to leave a single square inch of the planet under the control of the "unbelievers"—in other words, they are cultural chauvinists who see Sharia law as utterly superior to Western law, democracy, and principles of freedom. They believe a totalitarian Islamic culture would be Heaven on Earth—and that our free Western civilization, rooted in Judeo-Christian values, must thus be consigned to Hell.

Here we see one of the many contrasts between the Christian faith and the cult of the Islamists. From the seventh century to the present day, fundamentalist Islamists have readily resorted to conversion by conquest. If people are willing to voluntarily convert to Islam, fine. But Islamists do not hesitate to make converts—or eliminate unbelievers—by the point of a sword.

Unlike Islamists, Christians obey the Great Commission, the command of the Lord Jesus Christ to preach the gospel to all people in every nation. We call people to a saving faith in Jesus Christ—not by coercion but by invitation and conversion. Even though God does not want anyone to perish in their sins, he respects human free will and invites all to come to salvation *willingly and freely*.

JIHAD AGAINST THE WEST

For decades, Westerners in the United States and Europe were vaguely aware that the radical Islamists were "out there" somewhere—encamped in the Arabian desert, hiding in the mountains of Afghanistan and Pakistan, or destabilizing dictatorships in countries with unpronounceable names. The Muslim world always seemed remote and irrelevant to the daily lives of Westerners.

Occasionally, there would be some act of terrorism that would briefly attract the public's attention: the 1993 truck bombing in the basement of the World Trade Center in New York; the 1996 Khobar Towers bombing in Saudi Arabia that killed or injured many U.S. servicemen; the 1998 bombings of U.S. embassies in Kenya and Tanzania; the deadly Al-Qaeda attack on the USS *Cole* as it was refueling in Yemen. Yet even those attacks failed to convince Western leaders that jihadists were truly at war with the West.

Then came September 11, 2001—and everything changed. The scale, coordination, and sheer destructiveness of the 9/11 attacks caught the American national security community by surprise. For the first time, Westerners in general, and Americans in particular, realized that we are at war with a determined jihadist enemy.

Since then, jihadists have rained hammer blows on Western civilization, again and again. One of the most heinous and bloody attacks occurred in Paris on November 13, 2015, when Algerian-French ISIS gunmen entered the Bataclan Theater during a loud rock show, which meant that because of the noise, many in the crowd were slow to realize that they were under attack. The terrorists had made their way to a mezzanine and opened fire on the crowd below. They reloaded several times, threw hand grenades, and committed unspeakable acts of torture. When French tactical squads arrived, the terrorists triggered suicide vests, killing themselves and anyone close to them. The attack killed eighty-nine people and injured many more.

Did the government of France punish ISIS? No. The cowardly response of the leftist French government was to hide the awful truth from its own people—in part, to prevent a backlash against France's Muslim population. Finally, in July 2016, the government was forced to admit that the terrorists had committed unbelievably vile atrocities on their victims—so horrifying that one police investigator ran from the scene weeping and vomiting.[117]

Then, on Bastille Day, July 14, 2016, a Tunisian national with links to ISIS drove a heavy truck-trailer rig through a crowd on the Promenade des Anglais in Nice, France, the attack killing more than eighty people and injuring two hundred. Afterwards, French prime minister Manuel Valls declared a national state of helplessness, saying, "France must live with terrorism."[118] This statement stunned French citizens.

Following the attack, an American priest, Father Mark A. Pilon, observed that the collapse of European Christianity has rendered Europe incapable of responding to jihad:

> The dramatic loss of Christian faith in Europe is historically unprecedented. While some countries are slightly better off than others, the continent as a whole can no longer be described as a Christian civilization. . . .
>
> Even the latest horror of the beheading of an 85-year-old priest in Normandy and the revelations of the brutal tortures of victims in the Bataclan theater in Paris in November (finally leaked to the press) don't seem to have much raised understanding of the nature of the threat. . . .
>
> Europe is now almost godless, an almost totally secularized continent with little or no spiritual dimension in the various nations that constitute the European Union.[119]

Today's European leaders have no understanding of the historic conflict between the Christian West and the Islamic East. As Pilon explains, the leaders of Europe today are shrouded in the same spiritual blindness that Jesus described in Matthew 13:13—"they look but do not see and hear but do not listen or understand." In other words, Western leaders have not grasped the real nature of the existential threat we face from "the revival of a militant and determined form of extreme Islam bent upon, at long last, the domination of this formerly Christian continent."[120]

A THREAT THAT NEVER WENT AWAY

At Tours, France, in 732, a Christian army halted the First Jihad. That resounding Christian victory brought to an end the expansion of Islam into Christian lands for more than five centuries. Then, in 1683, a Christian army ended the Second Jihad outside the gates of Vienna—a victory that quelled the Islamic threat to Christianity for another two and a half centuries.

Now the Islamists have returned to the battlefield—and there are not enough Christians left to defend the gates of our civilization. The Islamists have declared jihad against the Western world. Their goal is the total surrender of all Western societies and submission to Sharia law.

The ideological forces that assaulted our civilization in 732 and 1683 have retreated but have never gone away. Radical Islam is relentless and patient in its pursuit of our destruction. Today, in the midst of the Third Jihad, we find that the Islamists are stronger than ever before, and yet Western culture is weaker and more vulnerable than ever before. This power imbalance is due to three undeniable factors:

FACTOR 1: THE ISLAMISTS HAVE DEMOGRAPHICS ON THEIR SIDE

The ultimate threat to Western civilization does not come from terrorism but from population dynamics. Both Europeans and Americans are having children at rates far below the replacement level—and so populations are dwindling. The combination of large-scale Muslim immigration into Europe and America, combined with the trend of large families among Muslim immigrants, guarantees that Western culture will recede as the immigrant Muslim culture expands.

You may think that because Muslims make up less than 2 percent of all Americans, and just 6.5 percent of people in the United Kingdom,[121] it will be a long time before radical Muslims become a majority voting bloc in the country. But radical Muslims don't need to become 51 percent of all voters in order to impose their will on society. Remember Wikipedia's list of British Muslim politicians in chapter 2? Despite being a tiny minority, Muslims are strongly represented at every level of the government in Great Britain.

Few Westerners realize that political influence isn't determined solely by the size of a voting bloc. Radical Islamists understand that there are a number of ways a minority group can achieve power and influence far beyond its numbers. Communities with strong cultural cohesion tend to have high voter turnout.[122] In the United States, Islamists are already concentrating their numbers in specific electoral districts (such as Minnesota's 5th District or Michigan's 13th District) to increase their political clout.

And, of course, radical Muslims form coalitions with the secular left, as Democratic Socialist mayoral candidate Zohran Mamdani has effectively done in New York City. By building alliances with leftists, Islamists amplify their voices and tilt the political game board in their favor. As a result of these and other strategies, radical Islamists are working hard to turn a small nucleus of committed voters into an outsized political force.

The Islamists, therefore, hope to conquer Western civilization at the ballot box, using the democratic process to abolish democracy. They have never wavered from their ultimate goal: to impose Sharia law on us, our children, and our grandchildren. If current trends continue, it's just a matter of time before Islam becomes the dominant culture, religion, and political system throughout the United States and Europe.

FACTOR 2: THE ISLAMISTS HAVE THE SECULAR LEFTISTS ON THEIR SIDE

Not only are the Islamists and the Progressive left joined together as co-equal branches of the Omnicause (as we saw in chapter 1), but Islamists know that Progressives will do anything to prove how "enlightened" and "inclusive" they are. Progressives are scared to death of being labeled "Islamophobic" and so, out of cowardice and an obsession with "political correctness," join forces with the jihadists who seek to destroy us.

Whenever leaders of the secular left actually tell the truth about the threat of political Islam, their fellow leftists pounce on them and cow them into submission. For example, in May 2025, Emmanuel Macron, the center-left president of France, directed his government to lay plans to stop the spread of political Islamism (especially the Muslim Brotherhood) in France. Macron called the Brotherhood "a threat to national cohesion." But the far left was quick to heap scorn on Macron, with Jean-Luc Mélenchon, leader of the leftist party La France Insoumise, tweeting of Macron: "Islamophobia has crossed a line."[123] Georgetown University professor Farid Hafez then went on to accuse Macron of "state-sponsored Islamophobia" and "racism,"[124] while Dr. Georgios Samaras of London's King's College decried "Macron's persistent anti-Islam narratives."[125]

As always, secular-left Progressives proved to be the Islamists' most vocal allies, the torrent of far-left condemnation leaving its mark on President Macron. On July 24, in an apparent bid to appease his critics, Macron announced, "France will recognize the State of Palestine."[126]

The world wondered: *What* State of Palestine? What is its capital? Who is the head of its government? What are its borders? Does it exist alongside the State of Israel—or in place of Israel? No one can say *because it doesn't exist*—but President Macron decided to recognize it anyway. Why? My guess is he is trying to persuade his Progressive and Islamist critics to stop bullying him.

U.S. Secretary of State Marco Rubio responded with dismay, saying that Macron's decision to recognize Palestinian statehood sank any possibility of hostage-release talks between Israel and Hamas. Even worse, Macron's declaration triggered a cascade of similar announcements from the leftist leaders of Canada, Australia, the United Kingdom, and Malta.

A senior Hamas official, Ghazi Hamad, stepped out of his luxurious hotel suite in Qatar to gloat to a reporter, "The initiative by several countries to recognize a Palestinian state is one of the fruits of October 7. We proved that victory over Israel is not impossible, and our weapons are a symbol of Palestinian dignity. . . . Without our weapons, no one would be looking in our direction. . . . We [Hamas] are the ones who brought the issue back to the forefront, and that is why all the countries are starting to recognize a Palestinian state."[127]

Ghazi Hamad got the message loud and clear from France, Australia, Canada, the UK, and Malta. These nations had *rewarded* Hamas for shooting, burning, beheading, and raping people to death, giving terrorists around the world a huge incentive to continue their jihad against the West. They proved that what the Islamists had always claimed is true: Western leaders are weak, cowardly appeasers who will hand over their civilization without a struggle.

FACTOR 3: THE ISLAMISTS ARE UNOPPOSED BY AN INEFFECTIVE, UNFAITHFUL CHURCH

Far too many Christians today are too timid or too compromised by the culture to take a firm stand for Jesus and his Kingdom. The further we move away from our biblical foundation, the more easily we drift into cowardice and confusion.

The threat that jihad poses to Christianity and the West is not a theoretical danger in the far-off future. It's here, it's now. Yet we seem blissfully unaware of the forces that threaten to engulf us. The Islamists are not only bent on conquering Western lands; they are determined to bring our minds and our souls, our children and our grandchildren, under the shadow of radical, political Islam. Their goal is to erase the gospel of Jesus Christ from our culture and to convert every church into a mosque.

But this is not the time for despair. We are citizens of the Kingdom of God. We should never allow world events, no matter how troubling, to darken our hearts or weaken our commitment to spreading the good news of Jesus. As the darkness grows, as the jihadists approach, let's seize this opportunity to shine the spotlight of God's love on the people around us. Let's illuminate the narrow pathway that leads to the Kingdom of Light.

The jihadists seem to be winning—but they haven't won yet. In the coming pages, we'll learn how to live boldly and victoriously for God's Kingdom.

5

AN INFLUENTIAL BUT LARGELY UNREAD BOOK

Al-Azhar University in Cairo, Egypt, is one of the oldest degree-granting universities in the world. It was founded around AD 970 by the Fatimid Caliphate as a center of Sunni Islamic learning. Though it offers courses in many fields of study, its courses in the Islamic religion and law are the most rigorous and challenging. To earn a degree in Islamic studies, a student must memorize and recite the entire Quran, which is nearly as long as the New Testament. Students must also be able to recite the Quran in its original Arabic with proper pronunciation and in a precise melody—a skill known as *tajweed*.[128]

What is the Quran, the most revered book in the Muslim world, and how did it come to be written?

THE WAR THAT OPENED THE WAY

In AD 602, the once-mighty Eastern Roman (or Byzantine) Empire went to war against the Sassanid Persians. The war dragged on until 628, when both empires were militarily worn out and financially bankrupt. At that time, a deadly contagion (probably bubonic plague) spread through both empires, killing thousands of people every day.

During the Byzantine-Sassanid War, on the Arabian Peninsula, events were taking place that were little noted by the two great warring empires. A man named Muhammad rose to prominence in Arabia and founded a religion. Today, that religion—Islam—is practiced by about two billion Muslims.

Muhammad was born in Mecca in around AD 570. At that time, the people of Arabia practiced various forms of idolatry, each tribe having its own pantheon of gods and nature spirits. For centuries, the Arabian people resisted efforts by Syrian and Egyptian Christians to convert them.

The family of Muhammad was the aristocratic Banu Hashim clan of the Quraysh tribe of Arabs. Muhammad's father died around the time of his birth and his mother when he was six, so he was raised by a grandfather and a paternal uncle. As a boy, he accompanied his uncle Abu Talib on a trading caravan to Syria, and it is on this journey that the young Muhammad heard stories from the Hebrew and Christian scriptures—stories now found, in heavily altered form, in the Quran.

As a young man, Muhammad led a merchant caravan to Syria on behalf of his distant relative, a wealthy businesswoman named Khadija. When he returned from his successful journey, forty-year-old Khadija was so impressed by his abilities that she asked the twenty-five-year-old Muhammad to marry her. Despite their difference in ages, he accepted her proposal. During their marriage, Khadija gave birth to two sons and a daughter. After her death, Muhammad took nine wives and several concubines.

Muhammad's journey to Syria on behalf of Khadija had a major formative impact on his beliefs. During that journey, Muhammad had many conversations with Syrian Christians, including a number of monks, and came away with many misunderstandings about the Christian message. The two biggest stumbling blocks in Muhammad's thinking were (1) the role of Mary and (2) the divinity of Jesus.

Sir William Muir wrote that the gospel Muhammad heard from the Syrian monks was tragically distorted. Muir wrote, "Instead of the simple majesty of the gospel—as a revelation of God reconciling mankind to himself through his Son—the sacred dogma of the Trinity was forced upon the traveler with . . . misleading and offensive zeal . . . and the worship of Mary [was] exhibited in so gross a form as to leave the impression upon the mind of Mahomet [Muhammad] that she was held to be a goddess, if not the third Person [of the Trinity] and consort of the Deity."[129]

Another influence on Muhammad was his wife Khadija's cousin, Waraqa, an Ebionite scholar in Mecca who had studied the Old and New Testaments. The Ebionites believed in Jesus as the Messiah and considered him a righteous prophet but not the Son of God—much as Muslims believe today.

Muhammad was offended by the pagan Arabs' belief that gods could have children with human women through sexual intercourse. Either the Syrian monks miscommunicated—or Muhammad misunderstood—the true meaning of the Christian doctrine of the Incarnation of Christ, which tells us that Mary's conception of Jesus was a miraculous work of the Spirit of God. Because Muhammad misunderstood the virgin birth, he rejected the doctrine of Jesus as the Son of God, and he insisted on calling Jesus "the son of Mary."

Influenced by the Hebrew and Christian stories he had heard, Muhammad rejected the idolatrous beliefs of the Quraysh tribesmen. He would sometimes go to a mountain cave to pray and, when he was forty, Muhammad claimed he was visited there by the angel Gabriel, telling his wife Khadija that God had called him to preach. She believed Muhammad's claims and supported him, though many in Mecca rejected his message. The revelations he preached about thus became the basis of the Muslim religion—and of the book known as the Quran.

Muhammad preached to the people of Mecca, calling them to turn from their idolatry and follow his new monotheistic religion. He attracted a few followers, but most of the people rejected his teachings. They scoffed at Muhammad because he was illiterate, but Muhammad claimed his illiteracy verified his story. He couldn't have read these revelations anywhere, he said, so he must have received them from Allah.

For thirteen years, Muhammad endured persecution in Mecca, his failure to win the hearts of the people troubling him deeply.

Finally, fearing for his safety, he left the city with his followers and moved to Yathrib, the city now known as Medina.

In Medina, the number of Muhammad's converts increased dramatically. He returned with his followers to Mecca in AD 630, fought the pagan tribes there, and conquered the city. Those early Muslims then destroyed all the pagan images in the city, with Muhammad declaring Mecca to be the holiest site of the Muslim religion and ordered that the city be closed to all non-Muslims—an edict that is still enforced today.

After conquering Mecca, Muhammad built up an army of 10,000 warriors and united the tribes of Arabia under the banner of Islam. Honored by his followers as a prophet of Allah, Muhammad's rise to power came at a favorable time for the rapid advance of his new religion. As historian George Liska observed, the "unnecessarily prolonged" Byzantine-Sassanid War thus created a power vacuum that "opened the way for Islam."[130]

THE CUBE IN THE COURTYARD

In the city of Mecca, there is a cube-shaped building made of black stone, known as the Kaaba. It stands at the center of Islam's most important mosque, the Masjid al-Haram—the holiest site in Islam. The Kaaba determines the *qibla*, the direction all Muslims face when they pray.

This cube-shaped building—the Arabic word *kaaba* literally means "cube"—existed for about a thousand years before Muhammad was born, and served as a shrine to the pagan deities worshipped by the Arab tribes. It stands in a broad courtyard in Mecca where the most important tribal deity worshipped was Hubal, a male god of divination.

After Muhammad entered Mecca in 630, he and his followers pulled down the statue of Hubal, along with all the other pagan idols. Then he dedicated the Kaaba to Allah, the monotheistic deity worshipped by the Muslims, making the Kaaba the central shrine of his new religion—and it is still the focal point of Islam today. Muslims call it "the house of Allah." When they make the pilgrimage to Mecca, they must walk around the Kaaba seven times, kissing and touching the Black Stone.

According to Islamic tradition, the Kaaba was constructed by Abraham and his son Ishmael. Muslims believe that when Ishmael's mother, Hagar, wandered in the desert with Ishmael, they reached the site where Mecca now stands. Both mother and son were nearly dead of thirst, so while Hagar searched for water between two hills, Ishmael rested under a shade tree. As the boy cried out in thirst and despair, water bubbled up under his feet, the spring unleashing a stream of flowing water. This spring became known as the Well of Zamzam, located just twenty yards east of the Kaaba. The well still supplies water drawn from a natural underground aquifer.

Islamic legend also claims that Abraham visited Zamzam to offer his son Ishmael as a sacrifice—a sharp contrast with the Genesis account, in which the son in the narrative is Isaac, not Ishmael, and the place is Mount Moriah, not Zamzam. Islamic tradition claims that after the angel stopped Abraham from sacrificing his son, Abraham and Ishmael built the Kaaba at the direction of Allah.

THE EVOLUTION OF MUHAMMAD'S MESSAGE

Muhammad's wife Khadija was his first convert, followed by Muhammad's slave Zaid, whom he later adopted as a son. His next converts were his two closest friends, Abu Bakr and Umar, who later succeeded him as leaders of the Islamic movement. Muhammad's fellow tribesmen in Mecca, however, refused to accept his message and they persisted in idol worship.

There was, however, a community of Jews in Mecca, and Muhammad befriended them. Some of the Jews even acknowledged Muhammad as a prophet, though most of the Jews tended to take a "wait-and-see" attitude. Muhammad incorporated many Jewish traditions and Old Testament stories into his new religion, and as a result, the Quran includes stories of Abraham and Ishmael, Hagar and Ishmael, Jacob and Joseph, and Lot and the destruction of Sodom and Gomorrah. These stories often differ from their biblical versions and are mingled with myths and legends from nonbiblical sources.

There was a step-by-step evolution of Muhammad's teachings. At each stage, he became increasingly more grandiose and extreme in his claims. At first, Muhammad claimed to bring warnings and a message of reform for the pagan Arabs of that region. He called upon them to turn to Allah, later equating his revelation with the revelations of Judaism and Christianity—and he placed himself on an equal plane with Moses and Jesus. Finally, he claimed that his new religion was God's final revelation, superseding both Judaism and Christianity.

In the end, Muhammad claimed that Islam was *the* universal faith—far superior to the Law of Moses and the gospel of Jesus. He claimed that Islam was the faith that began with Abraham (whom Muhammad called "the first Muslim"). He also claimed that this new message of Allah was announced in the Arabic language and was intended for Arabs, who would now have a prophet and a holy book of their own.

At first, the Jews in Arabia saw Muhammad as their ally. Muhammad warned against error and superstition—and so did the Jews. But, as Islam claimed to be superior to all other religions, the Jews backed away.

THE COMPOSITION AND CONTRADICTIONS OF THE QURAN

Muslims revere Muhammad as the *final* prophet of Allah in a long line of prophets. Islam acknowledges other prophets before Muhammad's time, including Abraham, Moses, David, and Jesus. Those other prophets, however, received an incomplete revelation, Muslims claim, whereas Allah gave Muhammad the complete and final revelation of truth. This ultimate revelation is found in the pages of the Quran, the collection of Muhammad's proclamations that his followers memorized and recorded.

Islam demands complete, literal obedience to the Quran. Islamic fundamentalists complain that the Quran has too often been interpreted figuratively by non-purists, which they see as a form of compromise and apostasy. According to Islam, every human being on Earth must submit to Allah's will, as it is explained in the Quran.

Fundamentalist Islamists are zealous when it comes to enforcing the Quran's laws on society, without compromise and without mercy. Are there "moderate" or mainstream Muslims who are less zealous and less extreme? Yes—but most dislike the term "moderate," which to them suggests compromise or lack of commitment. The term "moderate" is seen as reflecting a Western bias and even Western condescension. Many feel that the label "moderate" is a Western attempt to define Muslims by what they are *not* (extremist, Islamist, jihadist) rather than by what they *are*. Non-fundamentalist Muslims tend to prefer such terms as:

Progressive or Liberal Muslims—people who interpret the Quran and Islam in ways that are compatible with modern values and social reform.

Islamic Modernism or Centrism (*Wasatiyya*)—people who seek to reconcile Islamic faith with modern life while rejecting the interpretations of the fundamentalist extremists.

Cultural Muslims—people who are not deeply religious but identify with Islamic cultural heritage and tradition.

In this book, I will refer to such non-fundamentalist Muslims as "mainstream Muslims," because I believe they do represent the majority of Muslims in the world. Mainstream Muslims nevertheless have reason to be worried when zealous, extremist Muslims take control of society, simply because the freedom to interpret the Quran according to one's own conscience disappears under Islamist rule. Mainstream Muslims do not speak out against the excesses of the radicals and extremists because to do so means risking punishment and death.

The Quran is composed of 114 *suras* (chapters) that are arranged in order of length, beginning with the longest and ending with the shortest. Because they are not in chronological order, we don't know at which stage in Muhammad's life any given revelation came to him. Muhammad, being illiterate, did not write the Quran himself but spoke his revelations verbally for his followers to write down.

Muslim scholars have tried to arrange the events in the Quran in order. One Muslim scholar, Ibn Ishaq, gives this order: Creation; Adam and Eve; Noah and his offspring; Hud; Salih; Abraham; Lot; Job; Shu'ayb; Joseph; Moses; Ezekiel; Elijah; Elisha; Samuel; David; Solomon; Sheba; Isaiah; Al-Khidr; Daniel; Hananiah; Azariah; Mishael and Ezra; Alexander; Zechariah and John (the Baptist); the family of Imran and Jesus, son of Mary; the Companion of the Cave; Jonah; the Three Messengers; Samson; and George of Lydda (whom Christians call St. George). Clearly, then, the biblical characters mentioned in the Quran are not in historical order.

Muslims almost universally believe that the reason for the contradictions between the Bible and the Quran is that the Bible has been corrupted or altered. In fact, the real reason is Muhammad's vague and often erroneous understanding of the Bible. Here are a few of the differences between the Bible accounts and the stories of the Quran:

In the Quran's account of the flood of Noah, one of Noah's sons dies in the floodwaters and the Ark comes to rest on Mount Judi in Turkey (Quran 11:32–48). In the Bible, all members of Noah's family are spared, and the Ark comes to rest on Mount Ararat (Genesis 7:1–13 and 8:4).

In the Quran, the wife of Pharaoh rescues Moses from the river, saying, "It may be that he will be of use to us" (Quran 28:8–9). In the Bible, the daughter of Pharaoh spares Moses from the river out of compassion (Exodus 2).

In the Quran, the first miracle of Jesus is the making of a clay bird, then breathing life into it (Quran 3:49). In the Bible, his first miracle is turning water into wine at the marriage feast in Cana (John 2:11). (The second-century apocryphal book known as the Infancy Gospel of Thomas tells of Jesus, at age five, fashioning twelve sparrows from clay and breathing life into them, causing them to fly away.)

The Quran says of Jesus: "Christ the son of Mary was no more than a messenger" (Quran 5:75).[131] Although the Quran does state that Jesus was born of a virgin and lived a sinless life, it denies that Jesus is God in human form. By contrast, the Bible tells us that Jesus is the only begotten Son of God and the Savior of the world (John 3:16).

In the Quran, Jesus was not killed or crucified, but rather a likeness of Jesus *appeared* to be crucified (Quran 4:157)—in other words, the crucifixion was nothing but an illusion. This doctrine denies the historical evidence that Jesus of Nazareth really was crucified outside of Jerusalem at the order of Pontius Pilate. The crucifixion is a well-documented, well-attested fact of history, recorded not only in the Bible but in the histories of Flavius Josephus and Tacitus. The biblical accounts of the crucifixion, death, and burial of Jesus are found in Matthew 17, Mark 15, Luke 23, and John 19.

The Quran's denial of the crucifixion of Jesus, along with its denial of his claim to be the Son of God, is not merely a rejection of historical fact. It is a direct assault upon the gospel of Jesus Christ. They, for instance, deny the very *reason* for the crucifixion, which is that, on the cross, Jesus offered himself as an atoning sacrifice for our sins. The Christian concepts of atonement and salvation are not found in the Quran.

The author of the Quran appears unfamiliar with the core teachings of Christianity. Quran 5:72–75 and 5:116 suggest that the Christian conception of the Trinity consists of Jesus, Mary, and Allah. If the author of the Quran were truly God, wouldn't he have an accurate understanding of what Christians believe? As the all-knowing deity, Allah should possess complete knowledge of Christian doctrine. The Quran's inaccurate description of the Trinity is a serious problem for those who claim that the Quran is divinely revealed.

THE PRESERVATION PROBLEM OF THE QURAN

Many Muslims claim that the Quran has been flawlessly preserved without any variation throughout its history, but this claim is impossible to verify due to one significant historical event: the standardization of the Quran under the direction of Uthman, Islam's third caliph.

Uthman sought to unify the Quranic text by collecting it into a single, authoritative manuscript. He was concerned about increasing differences in recitation in different regions, which threatened to create confusion and discord within the Muslim community.

To address these concerns, Uthman gathered all existing fragments and oral versions, overseeing the production of a definitive standard codex. Upon completion of the standardized version, Uthman had all other versions burned. Not a fragment of any earlier manuscript is known to exist.[132]

This means it is impossible to know with certainty the exact wording of the Quran as it was originally spoken by Muhammad. The New Testament has no such problem. It exists in a wide array of manuscripts from many different regions, which enables scholars to study textual variations and seek the earliest form. Lacking such a diversity of early manuscripts, the original text of the Quran remains in doubt.

A LARGELY UNREAD BOOK

Few Muslims have read the Quran for themselves. Reza F. Safa, a former Shiite Muslim who converted to Christianity, once told an interviewer, "I have more knowledge of the Quran now than I ever did as a fanatical Muslim. Of all the Muslims I knew, only a handful had some knowledge of the Quran. And when I confront fanatical Muslims with the strange revelations of Muhammad in the Quran, they are unaware of these verses."[133]

There are several reasons Muslims do not read the Quran.

First, there is a high illiteracy rate among Muslims. In some Muslim nations, more than half the illiteracy rate ranges from 40 percent among men to 65 percent among women.[134]

Second, Muslims believe that the Quran must be read in Arabic, the language of Muhammad, but, according to the multi-faith website Learn Religions, only a tenth of all Muslims are native Arabic speakers.[135] Though there are translations of the Quran in other languages, only the original Arabic version is considered the genuine Quran. All other versions are considered interpretations, not reliable translations.

Third, reading the Quran is not required as a spiritual discipline in Islam. The Muslim religion is structured around the Five Pillars of Islam, which are drawn from different passages of the Quran.

Reading the Quran is not one of those Five Pillars. The five duties required of every good Muslim are:

1. The *Shahada* (confession of faith). Muslims must recite, "There is no God but Allah, and Muhammad is his prophet."
2. *Salah* (prayer). Muslims must pray, prostrate while facing Mecca, five times a day: before sunrise, after midday, at mid-afternoon, shortly after sunset, and in the fullness of night.
3. *Zakat* (paying the alms tax). The *zakat* or "purification tax" is levied on property. All Muslims pay this religious tax for the benefit of the poor.
4. *Sawm* (fasting). Muslims fast during the holy month of Ramadan, the month in which Muslims believe the first verses of the Quran were revealed to Muhammad. Between sunrise and sunset, adult Muslims do not eat, drink, or smoke.
5. *Hajj* (pilgrimage). Every Muslim who is physically, mentally, and financially able is expected to make a pilgrimage to Mecca during his or her lifetime. After making the pilgrimage, Muslims may add *al-Hajj* to their names.

All of this, of course, means that one can be a good Muslim without ever reading a syllable of the Quran—and most Muslims never do. They have never been challenged to read the Quran and have no interest in doing so.

But if Muslims never read the Quran, how do they know what it teaches? They let their religious teachers read it for them, interpret it, and explain it to them.

A BOOK, A LEGAL SYSTEM, A GLOBAL GOVERNMENT

Muhammad promised his followers the rewards of Paradise for those who died as martyrs in battle and plunder for those who prevailed in battle, promises that helped to secure his political leadership.

Throughout the Quran, Muhammad mapped out a framework for a theocratic government that governs every aspect of life.

The Quran covers such matters as dealing with enemies, the treatment of allies, the formation of treaties, and other political matters. It also maps out a code of conduct and a system of moral laws and requirements.

Alongside the Quran in the revered writings of Islam stands the Hadith—a collection of Islamic traditions, including stories and sayings of Muhammad as heard and remembered by his contemporaries. Many are second- or third-hand accounts of his words and deeds, along with sayings that explain the teachings of the Quran.

Toward the end of his life, Muhammad expressed his plans for the future expansion of Islam. He didn't want Islam to remain a purely Arab religion, but wanted to export Islam throughout the world. In 628, he dictated a series of letters and sent them to leaders of surrounding nations. He urged those leaders to convert to Islam, and through their leadership example, to convert their nations to Islam. He closed each letter with his personal seal that read, "Muhammad the Messenger of Allah."

According to Islamic tradition, Muhammad's letter to the Byzantine emperor read, "In the name of Allah, the most gracious, the most merciful, from Muhammad the Messenger of Allah to Heraclius the Emperor of Byzantium, greetings to him who is the follower of righteous guidance. I bid you to hear the divine call. I am the Messenger of Allah to the people. Accept Islam for your salvation." Muhammad sent similar letters to Cyrus, the Christian patriarch of Alexandria, Egypt; to Abd and Jaifar, the co-kings of Oman; to Ashama ibn Abjar, the king of Abyssinia; to Chosroes, the king of Persia; and to other religious and governmental leaders.[136]

In February 631, Muhammad declared a revelation from Allah that granted idolaters a four-month reprieve. Once this period elapsed, he proclaimed, Muslims were permitted to slaughter idolators and plunder their possessions, anywhere, at any time.

In March 632, Muhammad undertook his last pilgrimage from Medina to Mecca, accompanied by thousands of followers. Along the way, he instructed them in the rituals and requirements of the Hajj.[137]

About three months after this final pilgrimage, Muhammad was stricken with a severe headache; his legs were so weak and trembling that he couldn't walk without the support of his friends. His wives and his uncle suspected he might be suffering from pleurisy—a painful inflammation of the lungs—but Muhammad rejected this diagnosis, insisting that God would not afflict him with such a disease.

On June 8, 632, Muhammad died at the age of sixty-three. The religion he had established was then twenty-two years old.

When word of Muhammad's death spread, many Muslims were thrown into confusion and uncertainty. Abu Bakr, Muhammad's trusted companion and soon to be the first caliph of the Islamic community, told the mourners, "Whoever amongst you worshipped Muhammad, then Muhammad is dead, but whoever worshipped Allah, Allah is alive and will never die. Allah said: 'Muhammad is no more than an Apostle and indeed [many] Apostles have passed away before him.'"[138]

Muhammad's vision for Islam was that this new religion would infuse every facet of society, influencing every aspect of culture from attire to moral behavior to education to government to war and peace. The ambition among political Islamists today remains one of totalitarian control over the life of not only every Muslim but every human being.

6

ARE JEHOVAH AND ALLAH THE SAME GOD?

Patriarch Bartholomew (who was born Dimitrios Archontonis) is the Ecumenical Patriarch of Constantinople and the Primus Inter Pares (First Among Equals) of the Eastern Orthodox Church. On November 2, 2009, during a PBS interview with Charlie Rose, Patriarch Bartholomew said, "We are all created by the same God and as such we are brothers and sisters between ourselves. We have the same heavenly Father, whatever we call him."

Charlie Rose stopped him and asked, "All religions have the same heavenly Father?"

"Of course," Bartholomew replied. "God is but one, independently of the name we give him, Allah or Yahweh, and so on. God is one and we are his children and we have to love and understand each other."[139]

Though I admire and agree with Bartholomew's desire to see all members of the human family live together in peace and harmony, I do not agree that Allah and Yahweh (the God of the Bible) are one and the same God. And I can prove it by comparing the attributes of the God of the Bible alongside the attributes of the Islamic Allah.

COMPARING ALLAH TO JEHOVAH

The Quran lists ninety-nine attributes of Allah, known as "the most Beautiful Names" (*Asma al-Husna*). These names are not explicitly listed as a single set of ninety-nine names in the Quran but are derived from various verses and are widely recognized by Muslims.[140]

Christians would readily recognize many of the attributes of Allah, because they are also attributed to the God of the Bible: All-Powerful, Creator, the Merciful, the Compassionate. In Islam, however, the quintessential attribute of Allah—the one quality of Allah that overrides all others—is *power*.

You may have heard some defenders of Islam claim that it is "a religion of peace." Some have even claimed—wrongly—that the word *Islam* comes from the Arabic word *salam*, meaning "peace." But anyone with a knowledge of Arabic knows that *Islam* actually means "surrender" or "submission"—the word itself suggesting the surrender of a vanquished army, kneeling before a victorious conqueror. It speaks of the power of Allah to subjugate all his enemies, a call for human beings to surrender themselves to the all-powerful Allah.

The name Allah comes from pre-Islamic times. According to Middle East scholar E. M. Wherry, pre-Islamic Arabs worshipped many gods they called Allah. Pre-Islamic Allah worship involved worship of the sun, the moon, and the stars, which is why these cults are called "astral religions" (religions of the sky and stars). The crescent moon, which was an ancient symbol of pagan moon worship, is also the symbol of Islam, and you see the crescent moon on the flags of many Islamic countries, as well as atop minarets and mosques.[141]

The Quran describes the character of Allah as transcendent, merciful, wise, and all-knowing. Yet, in the narrative passages of the Quran, especially those that depict Allah's dealings with human beings, he appears to be remote, aloof, and distant.

Though the Quran describes Allah as merciful, wise, and all-knowing, it also portrays him as exalted far above humanity and transcendently unapproachable. While the Quran does speak of Allah's compassion, a close father-child relationship with Allah is beyond human reach. Allah's relationship with humanity seems closer to that between a stern but compassionate teacher and his pupil than that of a loving father and his child.

By contrast, both the Old and New Testaments depict God as a loving Father who is approachable and caring, and who wants to have a close relationship with his people. The God of the Bible walked and talked with Adam and Eve in the Garden of Eden. The psalmist wrote, "As a father has compassion on his children, so the Lord has compassion on those who fear him" (Psalm 103:13). In Hosea 11:1, God expresses his fatherly affection for Israel, saying, "When Israel was a child, I loved him, and out of Egypt I called my son."

In Ephesians 1:5, Paul writes that God the Father "predestined us for adoption to sonship through Jesus Christ, in accordance with his pleasure and will." In Matthew 7:11, Jesus tells us that God the Father wants to "give good gifts" to his children through prayer. And in Luke 15:11–32, Jesus vividly, compellingly illustrates the fatherly love of God through the many-layered Parable of the Prodigal Son. In that parable, Jesus illustrates the love, forgiveness, and welcoming embrace of God the Father—qualities that cannot be found in the Quran's depiction of Allah.

Jesus said, "Love your enemies" (Matthew 5:44; Luke 6:27–28). The Quran says, "Fight those who do not believe in Allah and the Last Day, nor comply with what Allah and His Messenger have forbidden, nor embrace the religion of truth from among those who were given the Scripture, until they pay the tax, willingly submitting, fully humbled" (Quran 9:29).[142]

The Bible says that all human beings are made in the image of God (see Genesis 1:27). In contrast, the Quran emphasizes Allah's otherness, making it clear that nothing is comparable to Allah—least of all, human beings. In fact, Quran 8:22 compares unbelievers to stupid animals: "Lo! the worst of beasts in Allah's sight are the deaf, the dumb, who have no sense" (that is, unbelievers, non-Muslims).[143]

This stark contrast between the biblical view of humanity versus the Quranic view may help explain why radical, political Islam places so little value on individual human lives, whether the lives of believers or unbelievers. This may also explain why, in its most extreme, radical, fundamentalist form, Islam easily becomes a death cult, whereas Judeo-Christian beliefs place a premium value on the life of every individual, because every individual is made in the image of God.

Jesus taught us that, instead of fighting and beheading our enemies, we are to pray for our enemies, do good to them, and "turn the other cheek" when they mistreat us. We do not demand that unbelievers convert to Christ at the point of a sword. We appeal to unbelievers to accept God's mercy and forgiveness through Christ. If they reject our gospel, we don't slay them—we pray for them and persevere in demonstrating the love of God.

CONTRASTING VIEWS OF TRUTH

Islam teaches that the angel Gabriel appeared to Muhammad and revealed Allah's will for the human race. Gabriel didn't give Muhammad any information about the nature, character, or personality of Allah. That's why Allah's nature in the Quran seems hidden and mysterious, whereas the God of the Bible is personal and knowable.

In the Bible, God speaks directly through a series of patriarchs and prophets. The God of the Bible reveals himself to humanity by telling us his names, and these names tell us about God's character and attributes. Here are just a few of God's names, as revealed in the Bible:

Adonai (Lord, Master)
El Shaddai (Lord God Almighty)
El Elyon (The Most High God)
El Olam (The Everlasting God)
Jehova Gmolah (The Lord Who Rewards in Full)
Jehovah Jireh (The Lord My Provider)
Jehovah Mekoddishkem (The Lord Our Sanctifier)
Jehovah Nissi (The Lord My Banner)
Jehovah Raah (The Lord My Shepherd)
Jehovah Rapha (The Lord Who Heals)
Jehovah Sabaoth (The Lord of Hosts)
Jehovah Shalom (The Lord Is Peace)
Jehovah Shammah (The Lord Is Present)
Jehovah Tsidkenu (The Lord Our Righteousness)

Islam and Christianity thus present very different pictures of who God is and how humanity should approach him. Although both Islam and Christianity call us to accept "by faith" what has been revealed by God, there is a vast disagreement concerning what has been revealed.

Islam claims that the ultimate truth was revealed by Allah to Muhammad through the angel Gabriel. Muslims explain the marked differences between the Bible and the Quran by claiming that text of the Bible has been corrupted over the centuries (a claim that has been proven false by textual criticism, paleography, archaeology, and historical linguistics), and claim that only the Quran contains the true divine message.

Christians contend that the ultimate truth was revealed through the life of Jesus Christ, who said, "I am the way and the truth and the life. No one comes to the Father except through me" (John 14:6). Jesus revealed God's truth through the way he lived his life as the incarnate Son of God. As John 1:14 tells us, Jesus is the *Logos*, the Word of God, the full expression of God's character, truth, and love toward humanity.

CONTRASTING VIEWS OF SIN

Many people are surprised to learn that the Islamic conception of sin is starkly different from the Christian and Jewish view. At first glance, however, much of what the Quran says about sin sounds almost biblical.

The Quran states that human beings were created for the service of Allah. Therefore, the root of sin lies in humanity's opposition to God's will. Humanity is prone to wrong actions because human beings are morally weak. So, if human beings do good works and obey Allah, their good works will cancel out their evil works. The Quran teaches, "Lo! good deeds annul ill-deeds. This is [a] reminder for the mindful" (Quran 11:114).[144]

Muslims reject the biblical view of sin, as stated by the apostle Paul: "For all have sinned and fall short of the glory of God" (Romans 3:23). They also reject the biblical view of human beings as sinners who desperately need a Savior, as stated by Paul: "For the wages of sin is death, but the gift of God is eternal life in Christ Jesus our Lord" (Romans 6:23).

According to Islam, Allah has given all people the ability to obey him and resist sin, and we only need to be guided into obedience. When a Muslim obeys the teachings of Islam, that obedience is seen as an expression of faith.

The Quran tells the story of Adam and Eve, but it does not include the concept of original sin that we find in the Genesis account. In Islam, Adam and Eve disobeyed Allah, but they repented and so Allah forgave them. Muslims believe that human beings are born without sin and with a natural inclination to obey God. According to Islam, human beings have free will, which can lead them to sin, but God is always willing to forgive those who sincerely seek it. According to the Quran, human beings have no need of a Savior.

Islam classifies various sins for the purpose of determining the degree of punishment those sins deserve. "Little sins"—*saghira*—include lying, deception, anger, and lust. Little sins are easily forgiven if the greater sins are avoided, and those little sins are offset by good deeds. In Islam, a lie may actually be a good deed if the lie is intended to help someone.

"Great sins"—*kabira*—include acts of murder, adultery, disobeying God, disobeying parents, getting drunk, practicing usury, neglecting Friday prayers, neglecting the fast of Ramadan, forgetting the Quran after reading it, swearing falsely or by any name but Allah's, performing magic, gambling, dancing, or shaving one's beard. Such sins can be forgiven only after repentant deeds.

Acts that the Christian Bible recognizes as sexual sins—adultery, fornication, prostitution—are often labeled in the Quran as acts of a "temporary marriage" rather than sin. In Islam, temporary marriage—known as *nikah mut'ah*—is a contractual marriage for a predetermined period, with a set dowry called a *mahr*. The length of the temporary marriage can range from hours to years. The Quran describes *nikah mut'ah* in Surah An-Nisa (Quran 4:24).

Students or migrant workers sometimes marry for a period of days, weeks, or months to obtain companionship and sexual release.

When the predetermined period is over, the marriage is dissolved without divorce. Temporary marriage thus often serves as a fig leaf for legalized prostitution but is not viewed as sin.

The worst sin in Islam is *shirk*, the association of other deities with Allah. The sin of shirk is unpardonable. According to tradition, Muhammad was asked to name the greatest sin and he said it was polytheism—the worship of more than one deity. Muslims believe that Christians are guilty of polytheism and shirk because they think that Christians worship three gods (the Trinity) rather than one. To the Muslim mind, the Christian sin of polytheism justifies waging holy war against Christians—unbelievers who have corrupted the true religion of Allah.

CONTRASTING VIEWS OF MERCY

Every chapter of the Quran except one opens with this phrase: "In the name of Allah, the merciful." Muslims believe that Allah's mercy is vast and is expressed through his forgiveness, compassion, and material blessings. And yet, though Islam teaches that Allah's mercy is vast, it also teaches that certain actions, attitudes, and beliefs can lead to a person being cut off from Allah's mercy.

The Quran proclaims repeatedly that Allah forgives sins, but the forgiveness of Allah is very different from the forgiveness expressed by the God of the Bible. Muslims believe that forgiveness is the sole prerogative of Allah—and the mind of Allah is unknowable, which means that a Muslim has no way of knowing for sure that his sins are forgiven.

As Christians, we have an abundance of promises and assurances of God's forgiveness: "As far as the east is from the west, so far has he removed our transgressions from us" (Psalm 103:12). "I, even I, am he who blots out your transgressions, for my own sake, and remembers your sins no more" (Isaiah 43:25). "Therefore, there is now no condemnation for those who are in Christ Jesus" (Romans 8:1). "In him we have redemption through his blood, the forgiveness of sins, in accordance with the riches of God's grace" (Ephesians 1:7).

Nowhere in the Quran can a Muslim find such hope and assurance. There are no promises of grace and forgiveness in the Quran that are like the promises of the Bible. A Muslim can only hope that, if nothing bad happens to him, then Allah must have forgiven him. Muslims live out their lives in the fear that one misstep, one missed prayer, one careless word might provoke Allah to consign him to Hell.

There is no atonement for sin in Islam. There are no sacrifices similar to the sacrifices in the Old Testament. There is no assurance of forgiveness and salvation in Islam like the assurances in the Christian gospel. Though Allah is called "merciful," he is stern and remote, and may dispense mercy or judgment at any moment, depending on his unknowable disposition.

DIFFERING VIEWS OF JESUS

Christians believe that Jesus is God's Son—that he is, in fact, God in human form. Muslims, however, completely reject the incarnation and divinity of Jesus. Islamic theology today reflects Muhammad's disgust with the idolatrous, polytheistic cults of pre-Islamic Arabia. He mistakenly thought that Christians believed in a God who married a human woman, Mary, who bore him a son, Jesus. Such stories were common among the polytheistic cults—and so Muhammad mistakenly saw Christianity as such a cult. His confusion is understandable in light of his illiteracy and his limited contact with Christian theology.

Though Muhammad rejected Christianity, he did claim that Jesus (called Isa in the Quran) was a prophet of God. Islam teaches that Jesus performed miracles, but they are not all the same miracles that we find in the gospel accounts. The Quran says that Jesus was born of a virgin, that he spoke from the cradle, that he breathed life into a clay statue of a bird, that he cured the blind and sick, that he raised the dead, that he spoke from hidden knowledge, and that he spread a table for his disciples with food from Heaven.[145]

Islam not only denies that Jesus is the Son of God but pronounces a curse on all who confess Jesus to be God's Son and the Lord of All. The Quran says, "And the Jews say: Ezra is the son of

Allah, and the Christians say: The Messiah is the son of Allah. That is their saying with their mouths. They imitate the saying of those who disbelieved of old. Allah (Himself) fighteth against them. How perverse are they!" (Quran 9:30).[146]

This verse critiques religious beliefs that stray from pure Islamic monotheism. The strong language of this verse ("Allah fights against them") emphasizes the seriousness of the sin of shirk in Islamic theology. Though mainstream Islamic scholars do not interpret this verse as a literal call to violence against Jews or Christians, some radical Islamists view this and other verses of the Quran as justification for hostility, war, and the killing of Islam's "enemies."

Muslims are baffled by the cross of Christ because they see no need of a sacrifice for sin. In fact, the Quran explicitly denies that Jesus was killed by crucifixion. Instead, it states that he was not killed by the Jews, nor was he crucified, but simply that it was made to appear that way.

Quran 3:54–55 claims that the enemies of Jesus plotted to kill him, but Allah confounded their schemes and took Jesus directly to Heaven: "And they (the disbelievers) schemed, and Allah schemed (against them): and Allah is the best of schemers. (And remember) when Allah said: O Jesus! Lo! I am gathering thee and causing thee to ascend unto Me, and am cleansing thee of those who disbelieve and am setting those who follow thee above those who disbelieve until the Day of Resurrection. Then unto Me ye will (all) return, and I shall judge between you as to that wherein ye used to differ."[147]

Many Islamic scholars claim that the image of Jesus was transferred to another man, who was then crucified in place of Jesus. Some suggest the crucified man was Judas Iscariot, others say Simon of Cyrene, while others say it was one of the disciples. Whatever the explanation, all Muslim teachers insist that Jesus was not crucified. This seems like a perfectly constructed, demonically inspired lie designed to keep Muslim people in spiritual darkness and blind them to the central truth of the gospel.

The Bible teaches that Jesus, out of love for us and obedience to the Father, humbled himself and submitted himself to death upon the cross. To a Muslim, this kind of self-sacrificing love is a sign of weakness. To love is to be vulnerable. Far be it from Allah, the all-powerful, to make himself vulnerable and submit to a humiliating death!

In Islam, God and human beings are wary of each other. In Christianity, God and human beings are in love with each other. Muslims cannot comprehend the power of divine love. They cannot understand a love that compelled God to take human form and live humbly among us so that we all might know who God truly is and what God is truly like.

ISLAM AND CHRISTIANITY: SIDE-BY-SIDE COMPARISON

Islam	*Christianity*
1. Allah/God	
Distant (unknowable).	Personal (knowable).
Does not reveal himself; reveals only his will.	Reveals himself through the incarnation of Jesus Christ.
Merciful (depending on his mood).	Loving (his love is unchanging).
Capricious (he leads and misleads).	Truthful.
Vengeful.	Just and compassionate.
Almighty (emphasis on power).	Almighty (power balanced by love).
2. Isa/Jesus	
A prophet.	God's Son.
Denial of the Incarnation.	The Word made flesh.
3. The Bible	
Revealed by Allah.	Revealed by God.
Changed and corrupted by unfaithful Jews and Christians.	Authoritative Word of God, preserved by the Spirit.

Islam	*Christianity*
4. Trinity	
God, Jesus, and Mary (Islam's distorted version).	Father, Son, and Holy Spirit; one God in Three Persons.
5. Faith	
Intellectual agreement that Allah is One and Muhammad is his Prophet.	Conviction that we are sinners and unable to save ourselves; we trust in Christ's substitutionary payment (atonement) for our sins.
6. Sin	
Rebellion against God. Result: shame, embarrassment. Dishonor to family. People are inherently good. We are absolved by good works.	Rebellion against God (primarily). Result: Guilt. Requires God's forgiveness. People are inherently fallen. The penalty of sin is death; Jesus alone paid the penalty for our sin.
7. Salvation	
God saves those whom he chooses. Faith and works are required. We cannot be assured of salvation.	Salvation is available to all who believe. Our works cannot save us. All who believe in Jesus will be saved.
8. Sanctification	
Based on rituals and obedience to the Quran. Keep the Five Pillars of Islam. External and ceremonial.	Based on our growth toward Christlikeness through the work of the Holy Spirit. Inward, spiritual, based on a living relationship with God.

Islam	*Christianity*
9. Love	
Islam recognizes erotic love and family love. Self-sacrificing love is seen as weakness.	Highest form of love is Christ-like, selfless *agape* love. Family love, friendship love, and erotic love have their place, but are secondary to *agape* love.
10. Belief in the Supernatural	
Belief in an unseen world. Angels (good and evil). Satan is a force of hate and power. Islamic belief is fatalistic; all events are foreordained by Allah.	Belief in a spiritual realm (Ephesians 6:12). Belief in angels and demons as described in the Bible. Satan is the rebellious arch-enemy of God, completely evil, but his power is no match for God's power. Human beings can overcome evil only through the power of God that is supplied by the Holy Spirit.

TWO RADICALLY DIFFERENT PRESCRIPTIONS FOR LIVING

As we compare and contrast Islam and Christianity, two facts become clear: First, Islam has adopted only bits and pieces of Old and New Testament teachings, and it has refashioned them into something distorted and unrecognizable. Second, despite a few superficial similarities, Islam and Christianity differ radically in how they portray the character of God, the state of humanity, and the way of salvation.

What do these differences mean? They offer two radically different prescriptions for living. The Christian gospel offers people a personal relationship with God through Jesus Christ. In Christianity, we have the absolute assurance that we stand cleansed and spotless before God because of the shed blood of Jesus Christ.

In Islam, there is no personal relationship with God. For the Muslim, good works are motivated by a fear of punishment that may be inflicted by a remote and impersonal God. The Muslim *hopes* to be acceptable to God because of his deeds—but he can never be sure he has done enough.

The differences between Islam and Christianity are thus profound. The Muslim view of Allah's character has a direct bearing on the ultimate expression of radical fundamentalist Islam—an expression we call terrorism.

7

WHEN CULTURES COLLIDE

Islamist terrorism is the most extreme and deadly manifestation of the Third Jihad. From the attack on the 1972 Summer Olympics by the Palestinian jihadist group Black September (which killed eleven Israeli athletes) to the September 11, 2001, attacks (nearly 3,000 dead at the World Trade Center, the Pentagon, and a Pennsylvania crash site) to the October 7, 2023, Hamas invasion of Israel (1,200 dead and many hostages kidnapped), senseless slaughter has been a favored instrument of the militants of the Third Jihad.

The origin of the Third Jihad can be traced to one man: Hassan al-Banna.

Born in 1906 as the son of a Sunni mosque teacher, Hassan al-Banna grew up fanatically devoted to fundamentalist Islam. When the Egyptian Revolution of 1919 erupted, he was thirteen years old and, despite his youth, took part in demonstrations and wrote political pamphlets supporting the revolution.

In 1923, Al-Banna enrolled at Dar al-Ulum College in Cairo and was shocked at the worldly, secular attitudes of many of his fellow students.

On March 3, 1924, the Grand National Assembly of Turkey abolished the Ottoman caliphate and sent the last Ottoman caliph, Abdülmecid II, into exile. The Assembly was carrying out the reformist agenda of the Turkish president, Mustafa Kemal Atatürk, who saw the caliphate as an obsolete relic of the past—a relic that prevented Turkey from becoming a modern, secular nation.

Everywhere Al-Banna looked, from his worldly fellow students to the secular Turkish government, he saw Islam in retreat. He knew that the Ottoman Empire had been steadily waning in power since the late 16th century, and had seen Ottoman Turkey suffer a humiliating defeat in World War I. He had sunk into despair over the abolishment of the Ottoman caliphate, viewing that moment in history as the symbolic end of the Islamic world's power and unity.

But Al-Banna refused to accept defeat, and decided to renew his commitment to Islamic principles. He was determined to re-establish the Islamic state, convinced that the revival of the caliphate was first priority of all true Muslims.

THE ORIGINS OF THE MUSLIM BROTHERHOOD

After completing his studies at a Dar al-Ulum in 1927, Al-Banna began teaching at an elementary school in the town of Ismailia, where the French-British consortium, the Suez Canal Company, was headquartered. To Al-Banna, the Suez Canal was a symbol of European colonialism, which he despised.

The canal had been built in the 1860s by a French-Egyptian partnership, but the expensive project had plunged Egypt into debt, which meant that Egypt was forced to sell its share in the canal to Great Britain (a lesson to all nations that pile up debt they cannot repay). The arrangement gave Britain seats in the Egyptian cabinet—and Egypt effectively came under colonial rule.

In 1928, Hassan al-Banna gathered six men around him, all Muslim Egyptians who worked for the Suez Canal Company and shared his hatred for colonial powers, for modernization, and for the diminishing influence of Islam in Egyptian society. Al-Banna and his six followers became the nucleus of an organization that became known as the Muslim Brotherhood. From this small beginning, the Muslim Brotherhood grew to an estimated two million members within two decades.

Hassan al-Banna taught his followers that the only way to defeat the corrupting influence of the West was to uphold Sharia law, based on the Quran. One of the key requirements of Sharia law is the establishment of an Islamic caliphate—a goal Al-Banna believed could only be achieved through armed struggle.

Al-Banna viewed with disgust any Muslim who watered down the warlike demands of the Quran and, in the late 1930s, he wrote a series of tracts advocating jihad. He warned Muslims against the growing belief that the jihad of the heart (the struggle against sin) is more important than the jihad of the sword. Citing the warlike passages of the Quran and the Hadith, he insisted that the most essential struggle Muslims faced was a struggle of the sword against unbelievers and colonial oppression. He thus urged his followers in the Muslim Brotherhood to prepare to shed blood. In one tract, he declared:

> Muslims . . . are compelled to humble themselves before non-Muslims, and are ruled by unbelievers. Their lands have been trampled over, and their honor besmirched. Their adversaries are in charge of their affairs, and the rites of their religion have fallen into abeyance within their own domains. . . . Hence it has become an individual obligation, which there is no evading, on every Muslim to prepare his equipment, to make up his mind to engage in jihad, and to get ready for it until the opportunity is ripe and God decrees.[148]

In 1939, Al-Banna and the Brotherhood's inner circle created a military wing called the Secret Apparatus. During World War II, the Muslim Brotherhood in Egypt and Palestine worked hand in hand with the Nazis. Its members organized mass demonstrations against the Jewish community in Palestine and helped distribute Arabic versions of anti-Jewish writings, including Hitler's *Mein Kampf* and the fabricated antisemitic document *The Protocols of the Elders of Zion*.

After World War II, the Brotherhood's Secret Apparatus carried out assassinations and terrorism against Jews, Christians, and Egyptian politicians. In December 1948, Prime Minister Nokrashy Pasha outlawed the Muslim Brotherhood, seized its assets, and sent scores of Brotherhood members to prison. This action provoked a student member of the Brotherhood to assassinate the prime minister.

In February 1949, Al-Banna arranged a meeting with Egyptian government officials to try to put an end to the bloodshed—but the officials never showed up. Instead, Al-Banna was ambushed and shot while waiting for a taxi. He later died from his wounds. The killers were never apprehended, but many people suspected that Egypt's King Farouk had ordered the assassination.

Hassan al-Banna, the founder of the Muslim Brotherhood, lit the spark for the Third Jihad, the current wave of global Islamic extremism. But another man poured kerosene on that spark and caused the Third Jihad to explode around the world. He would become an inspiration to such terrorist groups as Al-Qaeda and Islamic Jihad.

His name: Sayyid Qutb.

A JIHADIST IN COLORADO

Born in Egypt in 1906, Sayyid Qutb was a Sunni Muslim scholar and, in 1949, spent six months studying curriculum at Colorado State College of Education (now the University of Northern Colorado) in the typical middle-American town of Greeley. The people of Greeley were conservative, moral, mostly Christian people—in fact, Greeley was a "dry" town that banned the sale of alcohol.

You would think that a strict, fundamentalist Muslim like Qutb might approve of Greeley, with its conservative culture and prohibition of alcohol, but no—he actually saw the town of Greeley as a symbol of American decadence and depravity.

Raised in a dusty village in the central Egyptian desert, he was offended that Americans lavished gallons and gallons of precious water on their lush green lawns, which they manicured every weekend. He was offended by American support for the newly founded Jewish state of Israel. He was shocked that American women walked around town with their hair, arms, and even their knees exposed. He was also disturbed by the social injustice he saw in America in 1949, especially segregation.

Qutb's perspective on America was further distorted by his own social awkwardness. He never married, claiming he could not find a woman of "sufficient moral purity and discretion."[149] In this way, he was able to rationalize his clumsiness around women as a sign of spiritual superiority.

Writing in the Egyptian magazine *Al-Risala*, Qutb described American women as nothing but wicked, immoral jezebels: "The American girl is well acquainted with her body's seductive capacity. She knows it lies in the face, and in expressive eyes, and thirsty lips. She knows seductiveness lies . . . in clothes: in bright colors that awaken primal sensations, and in designs that reveal the temptations of the body—and in American girls these are sometimes live, screaming temptations! Then she adds to all this the fetching laugh, the naked looks, and the bold moves, and she does not ignore this for one moment or forget it!"[150]

Look at photos of how middle-American women dressed in 1949 and you'll understand that these are the words of a man projecting his own lusts and insecurities onto a foreign culture. Unwilling to acknowledge his own sinful urges, he condemns all of American womanhood.

Qutb's writings drip with condemnation for American manhood as well. He viewed men in America as brutal and obsessed with violent sports. And yet the odd "quirks" in this man's personality have profoundly shaped the thinking of jihadists ever since.

A NEW INTERPRETATION OF JIHAD

In 1953, Sayyid Qutb joined the Muslim Brotherhood and, through his influential writings, quickly rose to prominence as an intellectual leader and the editor of the Brotherhood's journal. In that role, he promoted a new interpretation of jihad, advocating for more militant, violent action.

Drawing on the 8th-century Salafism of Imam Ahmad Ibn Hanbal and the 18th-century Wahhabi Movement in Saudi Arabia, Qutb fundamentally reshaped Islamic political thought. (Salafism is a fundamentalist Sunni movement that embraces the practices and dogmas of the earliest Muslims, including Muhammad himself, who were known as the Salaf. The Salafis, such as Sayyid Qutb, believe they practice the purest form of Islam.)

Traditional Islamic law emphasized order and stability, and prohibited rebellion against Muslim rulers. But Qutb reinterpreted Shariah law to provide a religious justification for overthrowing Muslim rulers who (in his view) had strayed from pure Islamic principles. It was this new interpretation that opened the door for the Muslim Brotherhood to assassinate Muslim leaders and overthrow Muslim governments that they viewed as insufficiently zealous for Islam. He also redefined jihad to include not only defensive violence but terrorism and armed struggle in order to establish Allah's authority on Earth.

Qutb condemned Western ideals of freedom, democracy, and human rights as incompatible with Islamic law, and so he divided the world into two conflicting cultures: Islam and *jahiliyya* (pre-Islamic ignorance). He urged Muslims to return to pure seventh-century Islam, saying, "We need to initiate the movement of Islamic revival."[151] His views spread rapidly and still assert a towering influence over the Muslim world today.

Sayyid Qutb has been called "the father of modern [Islamic] fundamentalism" and "the most famous personality of the Muslim world in the second half of the twentieth century,"[152] his writings profoundly shaping the thinking—and terrorist actions—of Osama bin Laden and Ayman al-Zawahiri.

After the dictator of Egypt, Gamal Abdel Nasser, survived an assassination attempt by a Muslim Brotherhood gunman in 1954, the Egyptian government arrested thousands of Brotherhood members, including Qutb, who was convicted of being a key player in the Brotherhood's outlawed Secret Apparatus.

In prison, Qutb wrote his manifesto, *Ma'alim fi al-Tariq* (*Milestones*), which was smuggled out of the prison by friends and secretly published. Though the Egyptian government banned his writings, it was unable to suppress them, and his writings became widely circulated throughout the Islamist underground.

Though Qutb was originally sentenced to life in prison, his sentence was reduced due to poor health. Only six months after his release, he was, however, arrested again for plotting against the Egyptian government. After being convicted and sentenced to death, Qutb told the court, "I performed jihad for fifteen years until I earned this martyrdom."[153]

Sayyid Qutb was executed by hanging on August 29, 1966, but his martyrdom only magnified his legend among his fellow jihadists. His influence has grown so strong that his ideology has become known as Qutbism (or Qutbiyya), a radical fundamentalist form of Sunni Islamist ideology. His writings continue to be studied across the Muslim world, from Morocco to Malaysia.

Whenever a jihadist commits a terrorist attack in the Western world, that attack can logically be traced to two 20th-century Muslims: Hassan al-Banna and Sayyid Qutb. Both started out small, and yet from these humble beginnings have come swarms of jihadists who continue to assault the towers and foundations of Western civilization to this day.

WHY ISLAMISTS HATE CHRISTIANITY

Jihadists hate everything Christians love—the gospel of Jesus Christ (which is blasphemy to their ears), America's First Amendment freedoms, and our tolerant society, which values liberty and diversity. They envision the entire world in submission to Sharia law. There are five reasons jihadists see Christianity as the greatest enemy of Islam:

1. Because of the history of the Crusades, jihadists consider Christianity their most formidable ideological adversary. Many Muslims still refer to Christians and Westerners as "Crusaders" to this day.
2. Radical Islamists blame Christianity for the unbelief and moral corruption they see in the West. They mistakenly believe that Christian values dominate Western society, just as Islamic principles shape life in Muslim-majority countries. Unfamiliar

with Western secularism and diversity, they often attribute the rampant immorality in American music and Hollywood films to Christianity itself.

3. Jihadists see Christians as docile and easily cowed into submission. They perceive Western tolerance as a sign of weakness—a character flaw they can exploit to bully Western society into surrender. The eagerness of Western leaders (like Emmanuel Macron of France and Keir Starmer of Great Britain) to appease radical Islamists reinforces this perception, as does their reluctance to defend Western cultural values.
4. Radical Islamists attribute a long list of Middle Eastern social ills—poverty, hunger, instability, oppression—to the Christian West. They hold the West responsible for undermining Muslim culture and offending Muslim honor through the spread of anti-Muslim ideas.
5. Islamists blame the West for its support of the Jewish state of Israel.

As a result, while Jesus teaches us to love our enemies, the Quran gives radical Muslims permission to wage war against their enemies:

"Fight against such of those who have been given the Scripture as believe not in Allah nor the Last Day, and forbid not that which Allah hath forbidden by His messenger, and follow not the Religion of Truth, until they pay the tribute readily, being brought low" (Quran 9:29).[154]

"And slay them wherever ye find them, and drive them out of the places whence they drove you out, for persecution is worse than slaughter. And fight not with them at the Inviolable Place of Worship until they first attack you there, but if they attack you (there) then slay them. Such is the reward of disbelievers" (Quran 2:191).[155]

"O ye who believe! Take not the Jews and the Christians for friends. They are friends one to another. He among you who taketh them for friends is (one) of them. Lo! Allah guideth not wrongdoing folk" (Quran 5:51).[156]

"They surely disbelieve who say: Lo! Allah is the Messiah, son of Mary. The Messiah (himself) said: O Children of Israel, worship Allah, my Lord and your Lord. Lo! whoso ascribeth partners unto Allah, for him Allah hath forbidden paradise. His abode is the Fire. For evil-doers there will be no helpers" (Quran 5:72).[157]

Today, the clash between Christianity and Islam can be traced back to the era of Muhammad himself. Islamists have revived all the old hostilities, and are at war against "Crusaders" and "infidels." The nerve center of jihadism in the world today is the transnational Islamist organization founded by Hassan al-Banna and energized by Sayyid Qutb—the Muslim Brotherhood.

HOPE ON THE HORIZON

A few years ago, while I was visiting a Middle Eastern nation, I met with a highly placed Muslim official. As we talked, he leaned toward me and said, "Dr. Youssef, can you tell me why the Muslim Brotherhood is outlawed as a terrorist organization in Saudi Arabia, Bahrain, the United Arab Emirates, and Egypt—but is allowed to flourish in America and the West?"

I shook my head and said, "I can think of no answer except foolishness and ignorance."

This powerful leader, a Muslim himself, saw the Muslim Brotherhood as a threat not only to Western civilization but even to the stable order of Muslim countries like his own. He could not understand why the United States permitted such a threat to operate within its own borders.

Yet there are signs that America's casual attitude toward the existential threat of the Muslim Brotherhood may be changing. Texas Senator Ted Cruz has been trying for more than a decade to have the Muslim Brotherhood officially designated a terrorist organization. He introduced a series of Senate bills to make that designation, but critics blocked each one. His opponents argued that only *some* branches of the Brotherhood are violent, so it would be wrong to condemn the *entire* organization.

I would suggest that such a view of the Muslim Brotherhood is the equivalent of making a stew out of beef, carrots, potatoes, and onions, seasoned with poisonous hemlock and deadly nightshade.

The vast majority of the ingredients are wholesome and perfectly healthy, so it would be wrong to condemn the entire stew because of a few toxic ingredients, wouldn't it? I'm glad Senator Cruz sees the Brotherhood for what it truly is—and that he's taking strong action, despite opposition from the Brotherhood's far-left allies.

On July 16, 2025, Senator Cruz announced a new version of his Muslim Brotherhood Terrorist Designation Act, and was joined by Senators Tom Cotton (R-Ark.), John Boozman (R-Ark.), Rick Scott (R-Fla.), Ashley Moody (R-Fla.), and Dave McCormick (R-Pa.). Representatives Mario Díaz-Balart (R-Fla.) and Jared Moskowitz (D-Fla.) have also introduced companion legislation in the House.[158]

When Senator Cruz announced the new bill, he said, "The Muslim Brotherhood is a terrorist organization, and it provides support to Muslim Brotherhood branches that are terrorist organizations. One of those branches is Hamas, which on October 7 committed the worst single-day massacre of Jews since the Holocaust, which included the murder and kidnapping of at least 53 Americans."

Cruz added that the Brotherhood "poses an acute threat to American national security interests. American allies in the Middle East and Europe have already labeled the Brotherhood a terrorist organization, and the United States should do the same, and do so expeditiously."[159]

Leftists and Progressives seem incapable, however, of grasping the worldview of the Brotherhood, especially its willingness to patiently pursue its dreams of conquest over a span of generations. The Muslim Brotherhood starts with influencing public opinion and government policies but will use any means, including subversion and terrorism, to dismantle Western societies. Senator Cruz's legislation would expose the Brotherhood's true nature and help disrupt its financial and propaganda networks.

Dr. Lorenzo Vidino, director of George Washington University's Program on Extremism, explained why Senator Cruz's legislation is urgently needed. "The Brotherhood is a very nefarious group," he said, adding, "It's not black and white; it's very gray. . . . The fact they have this ability to present themselves as moderate . . . makes them way more dangerous in the long term. Nobody in Congress would meet with ISIS or Al-Qaeda, but they do [meet] with the Brotherhood."[160]

Senator Cruz's bill is a necessary step. But it's only one step. We have a long way to go to prevent the jihadists from achieving their objective—the fall of our civilization and the establishment of a global caliphate.

8

THE GOAL OF A GLOBAL CALIPHATE

In June 2024, the Dissident Dialogues festival in New York City was the site of a fascinating public conversation between Ayaan Hirsi Ali and her longtime friend, atheist champion Richard Dawkins. Ayaan Hirsi Ali is a thoughtful, articulate Somali-born woman who has journeyed from Islam to atheism and finally to Christianity.

When the moderator asked Ali to explain why she had converted to Christianity, she explained, "I had a personal crisis. I lived for about a decade with intense depression and anxiety and self-loathing . . . I actually didn't want to live anymore, but wasn't brave enough to take my own life. So I was self-medicating . . . Having reached a place where I had absolutely nothing to lose, I prayed and I prayed desperately. And for me, that was a turning point . . . I now feel connected to something higher and greater than myself. My zest for life is back."

"Ayaan," Dawkins said, "that's a moving personal story. But . . . a Christian has to believe in something. You go to church now and listen to the vicar. Do you notice what a lot of nonsense he talks? I mean, do you really take it seriously that Jesus is the Son of God? That Jesus rose from the dead? . . . That is a part of Christianity."

Ali replied, "I know you very well. We've been friends for a long time. In fact, in some ways, I think of you as a mentor. You're coming at this from a place of: 'there is nothing.' What has happened to me is I have accepted there is Something . . . God turned me around . . . It makes a great deal of sense."

Richard Dawkins was dumbfounded. He knew that Ayaan Hirsi Ali possessed a formidable intellect, and had seen her deliver many devastating arguments for atheism in debates against believers. He couldn't understand how she could completely switch sides and become a Christian. In a bewildered tone, he said, "You don't believe Jesus rose from the dead? Surely?"

"I choose to believe," she said, "that Jesus rose from the dead . . . I choose to have faith, because of what I've experienced."

"I came here," Dawkins said, "prepared to persuade you, Ayaan, that you're *not* a Christian. But I think you *are* a Christian. And I think Christianity is *nonsense*."

He went on to compare Islam and Christianity. "Islam is a nasty religion," he said. "I think we agree about that. But Christianity is not all that nice either. Christianity is obsessed with sin."

Ali gently disagreed. "I find that Christianity is actually obsessed with love," she said. "It's a message of redemption. And it's a story of renewal and rebirth."

She compared the sense of peace and assurance she had as a Christian with the fear she lived with every day when she was a Muslim. "I was taught," she said, "that the only way to be faithful is to have fear—naked fear—and to have these sets of obligations which you must obey."

Ali went on to worry aloud that an entire generation of young people had been infected by two "mind viruses"—far-left woke-ism and Islamism. "There are mosques and Islamic centers," she said, "that have convinced young people here in America and in Britain and elsewhere that Christianity is dead and has nothing to offer—that Western civilization is a moral vacuum, and that they're here to fill it . . . You have this amazing civilization, you have this amazing society, and it is pretty frightening to see that the best and the brightest are converting to the mind virus of woke-ism and the mind virus of Islamism."[161]

This is so true. Our Judeo-Christian values have given us an amazing civilization. These values have given us a society structured around the blessings of freedom. Yet we are just a generation away from seeing it all turn to dust as young people are lured by these twin "mind-viruses": woke-ism and Islamism.

Western civilization prizes liberty, tolerance, progress, compassion, and peace, while militant Islamists demand submission to an ancient and merciless code of theocratic laws. Their worldview is a throwback to the 7th century—yet oil wealth and 21st-century Western technologies have given them the power to destabilize and conquer our civilization.

In all the centuries since Muhammad founded the Muslim religion, one thing has never changed: Islam's goal of world domination.

DREAMS OF A WORLD EMPIRE

What would a global Islamic empire look like? How would it treat its citizens? We don't need to wonder or speculate. We simply have to study history.

After the death of Muhammad in 632, the Muslim empire—driven primarily by armed conquest—expanded rapidly. Abu Bakr, the first caliph, consolidated Islamic control over the Arabian Peninsula through the Ridda Wars (632–633), which the Muslim armies fought against rebellious Arabian tribes. Abu Bakr's forces won every battle and demanded that the defeated tribes swear allegiance to Islam.

Abu Bakr was succeeded by Umar ibn al-Khattab, the second caliph, who continued Islam's rapid territorial expansion. Umar ruled for ten years, from 634 until his assassination in 644. Under Umar, Muslim armies expanded the Muslim empire to include vast territories once controlled by the Byzantine and Sasanian (Persian) empires. Umar conquered the Levant (Syria, Jordan, Lebanon, and Palestine, including Jerusalem), Mesopotamia (Iraq), Persia (Iran, Azerbaijan, Armenia, Georgia), Egypt, and parts of Afghanistan, Turkmenistan, and southwestern Pakistan. Historian James Buchan observed, "In speed and extent, the first Arab conquests were matched only by those of Alexander, and they were more lasting."[162]

Within a hundred years after Muhammad's death in 632, the Muslim empire stretched as far west as Spain and as far east as India. Although the empire began to crumble in some regions by the late 900s, Islam experienced a resurgence around the 1400s with the rise of three new and powerful empires: the Mughal Empire in India, the Safavid Empire in Iran, and the Ottoman Empire in Anatolia (Turkey). And so it was that Islam penetrated deeply into Africa, Asia, and the Middle East, with millions converting to Islam, either willingly or at sword-point.

The Ottoman Empire was the most aggressive of the three Islamic movements, and by the end of the 1500s, the Ottomans had conquered several Byzantine provinces, including Greece and Bulgaria. Constantinople, long a bulwark of Christendom, fell in 1453. The Muslim conquerors renamed it Istanbul and made it the capital of the Ottoman Empire.

Under Suleiman the Magnificent, who reigned from 1520 to 1566, the Ottomans gained control of most of the Balkan Peninsula, encircled the Black Sea, controlled Asia Minor, the Euphrates valley, Armenia, Georgia, Syria, Palestine, and northern Africa from Egypt to Morocco. By the 16th and 17th centuries, the Ottomans had conquered much of southeastern Europe, including Greece, Serbia, and parts of Hungary, the empire's march through Europe ending only with the siege of Vienna in 1683.

During the centuries-long reign of the Ottoman Empire, many once-Christian regions became predominantly Muslim, with forced conversion to Islam commonplace. Churches were converted into mosques, and sons of Christian parents were ripped from their homes, brainwashed into the Muslim religion, and conscripted into the armies of Islam.

ISLAM AT WAR WITH ITSELF

The Muslim-versus-Muslim violence that continually roils the Middle East is bewildering to most Westerners. Why are Muslims so often fighting and killing other Muslims?

The Yemen Civil War, for example, is a struggle involving multiple factions and splinter groups, all of them Muslim. The two main sides of the conflict are (1) the internationally recognized Sunni government of Yemen, and (2) the Houthi Rebels, a Shia group also known as Ansar Allah or "the Supporters of Allah."

The conflict began in September 2014 with a series of Houthi-led protests and street battles, leading to the Houthis seizing the presidential palace in Sanaa, the capital of Yemen, in January 2015, with Yemen's president, Abd Rabbu Mansour Hadi, fleeing to the port city of Aden, hoping to maintain his rule. On March 25, the Houthis reached Aden, forcing Hadi and his advisors to flee Yemen altogether. That same month, a coalition of Gulf states, led by Saudi Arabia, launched a campaign of air strikes against the Houthis. Hadi set up a government-in-exile in Saudi Arabia, where he remains to this day.

The Houthis take their name from the founder, Hussein al-Houthi, who died in 2004. His brother, Abdul-Malik al-Houthi, now leads the group. Despite being a Shia minority in a Sunni-majority nation, the Houthis have continued to administer the city, collect taxes, and even print money. They have been well supplied by Iran with a powerful arsenal, including missiles that they have lobbed into Israel or fired at oil tankers and American warships in the Red Sea.

Houthi rule in Yemen has caused a nationwide humanitarian crisis, with an estimated 11 million children facing starvation. The goal of the Houthis is to gain complete control of Yemen and launch attacks against the United States, Israel, and Saudi Arabia.

The war in Yemen is further complicated by the presence of other Muslim factions, all vying for power. There are, for instance, the Yemeni southern separatists known as the Southern Transitional Council, which seeks independence for southern Yemen. Al-Qaeda in the Arabian Peninsula (AQAP) also operates in Yemen, and there are many local Muslim tribes that align with one side or another, based on their own provincial interests. The war is complicated—but it largely comes down to a struggle between the Shias (Houthis) and the Sunnis (the Hadi government).[163]

FOURTEEN BLOOD-DRENCHED CENTURIES

The split between the Sunnis and Shias goes all the way back to the earliest years of Islamic history following a dispute over the question of who should succeed Muhammad after his death in 632. Nearly fourteen centuries since the dispute began, Muslims are still killing Muslims by the tens of thousands. Here's how it all began:

After Muhammad's death in 632, the central issue was whether leadership should pass through the Prophet's family or be determined by merit and consensus within the broader Muslim community. Sunnis held that the caliph ought to be selected by the community's prominent members based on their leadership reputation. The Sunnis supported Abu Bakr, a close companion of Muhammad, as Islam's first caliph, but the Shiites insisted that leadership belonged to Muhammad's family—specifically to his son-in-law, Ali ibn Abi Talib.

Predictably, these irreconcilable differences led to an intense power struggle that laid the groundwork for a lasting hatred between the Sunnis and Shias—and a history drenched in blood.

The Sunni-Shia struggle erupted in warfare at the Battle of Karbala, Iraq, in October 680 when Imam Hussein, grandson of the Prophet Muhammad, who embraced the Shia interpretation of Islam, led a small force of fewer than a hundred men. They faced a much larger force led by the Umayyad caliph Yazid I, who embraced the Sunni interpretation, with his army numbering at least 4,000 men (Shia sources claim it was closer to 30,000 men).

Imam Hussein delivered a speech to his enemies, demanding safe passage and reminding the forces of Yazid that he was the grandson of Muhammad himself. In turn, Yazid's forces said he would be allowed to leave, but only if he pledged his allegiance to the caliph, Yazid. Naturally, Hussein refused—and so the battle began. It was a bloody onslaught of cavalry charges, archery volleys, and sword duels, and when the Battle of Karbala was over, Imam Hussein and most of his companions were dead.

Though the terms "Sunni" and "Shia" had not been formalized at that time, the battle crystallized the divisions between the two great factions of Islam. One faction was the *Shi-at Ali*—literally "the party of Ali," which supported the descendants of Ali as the rightful rulers of the Islamic world. These became known as the Shias or Shiites. The other group became the Sunnis, the "followers of the Prophet's Path," supporters of the Umayyads and later the Abbasids.

Shias and Sunnis share core tenets; they both, for instance, revere the Quran and the Five Pillars of Islam. And yet, despite these shared doctrinal beliefs, Shias and Sunnis are mortal enemies to this day.

A RELIGIOUS DUTY TO KILL

Shias believe that the descendants of Ali, the Imams, are sinless and virtually infallible leaders in both the religious and political spheres of life. To Shias, the Imams are thus the only people capable of properly interpreting the Quran.

The Twelver Shias sect teaches that the infant Twelfth Imam went into occultation (a mysterious state of hiddenness) during the ninth century and will remain hidden until the end of time, when he will return to Earth as the *Mahdi*, a Messiah-like figure who will establish a millennium of global justice and peace. Until the Twelfth Imam returns, Twelver Shias believe, every true Muslim must put himself under the authority of an *ayatollah* (holy man)—who wield enormous power and authority over the people—and it is this belief that has given rise to a strong clergy and a rigid religious hierarchy within the Twelver Shia sect.

In 1501, Twelver Shia Islam became the official religion of Persia (now Iran) with the rise of the Safavid dynasty, the Shia clergy demanding that the state give allegiance and obedience to the clergy. In 1906, the Shia clergy in Persia led a revolution that established a constitution and caused the fall of the two-hundred-year-old Qajar dynasty. This gave rise to the first Pahlavi Shah, Reza Shah.

In Iran, the Ayatollah Ruhollah Musavi Khomeini played on the Twelver Shiites' expectation of the return of the Twelfth Imam. Claiming to be a linear descendant of Ali, he encouraged his followers to believe he was the long-awaited Mahdi. He led the 1979 Iranian

Revolution, which overthrew Mohammad Reza Pahlavi, the Shah of Iran. Then Khomeini set up a new revolutionary government, giving the clergy absolute authority.

The Ayatollah Khomeini was, however, also determined to export his theocratic form of government to other nations, and so he called for the downfall of Saddam Hussein, the Sunni dictator of neighboring Iraq. The result was the eight-year Iran-Iraq War, in which Iran sent every able-bodied male into battle, some as young as thirteen.

Both nations paid a heavy toll for the war, which lasted from September 1980 to August 1988, with roughly a million Iranians and 300,000 Iraqis killed or wounded. In fact, the high cost of the war may have been what led Saddam Hussein to invade oil-rich Kuwait on the pretext that Kuwait was the "nineteenth province" of Iraq.

That invasion, in turn, led to the Persian Gulf War, from 1990 to 1991, with the United States leading an international coalition in Operation Desert Storm, which liberated Kuwait.

The history of Islam thus shows that, almost since its inception, Islam has been at war with itself. Century after century, caliphs and imams and warriors have battled each other and killed each other to prove themselves the purest, most righteous Muslims of all.

THE TOTALITARIAN IMPACT OF ISLAM

Soon after seizing power in Iran, the Ayatollah Khomeini declared, "The governments of the world should know that Islam cannot be defeated. Islam will be victorious in all the countries of the world, and Islam and the teachings of the Quran will prevail all over the world."[164] Khomeini was, however, simply restating what Muslim leaders have declared for centuries: Islam is a worldwide movement that seeks global dominance.

What happens when an Islamic government takes power? We invariably see three consequences that impact the lives of Muslims and non-Muslims alike.

First, *the Islamic government abolishes personal freedoms.* Islam knows nothing of such notions as "live and let live" or "to each his own." It demands absolute submission and, once political Islam takes control, personal freedoms disappear. All symbols of non-Muslim culture must be erased, and everyone becomes subject to Sharia law.

During the twenty-year American occupation of Afghanistan, from October 2001 to August 2021, Afghan women and girls could go to school, get jobs outside the home, engage in women's sports, and have access to healthcare and the justice system. After the United States withdrew, all of that ended.

The Taliban rushed in to impose its seventh-century ideology, and gun-toting Talibs reimposed strict Sharia law. Those who broke the rules faced arbitrary arrests, forced disappearances, torture, amputations, floggings, and public executions, with the Taliban targeting former government officials, journalists, professors, and anyone suspected of having helped the Americans.[165]

This is the "paradise" the Islamists plan to impose on the world.

Second, *the Islamic government puts an end to innovation*. Under Muslim rule, modernization and technological advances come to a halt. (One exception is weapons technology—such as Iran's attempt to develop nuclear weapons and missiles.) Except for oil-rich nations like Iran, Saudi Arabia, the UAE, and Qatar, most Islamic nations are poor—wealth in the modern world is generally the result of modernization, to which Islam is traditionally opposed.

There's a saying that the Hadith attributes to Muhammad: "The truest word is the Book of Allah, and the best guidance is the guidance of Muhammad. The most evil matters in religion are those that are newly invented, for every newly invented matter is an innovation, every innovation is misguidance, and every misguidance is in the Hellfire."[166] This cautions against *religious* innovation, but the distrust of innovation *in principle* is such an accepted article of Islamic faith that it pervades all of society and all forms of innovation.

Enough Western innovation has, however, trickled into the Islamic world to show poor Muslims that they are being deprived of the conveniences and prosperity of the West. Muslims thus feel they are missing out on the blessings of the 21st century—but do they blame the backward ideas of their Islamist leaders? No, they blame the West. Their leaders tell them, "The reason you live in poverty is that the Great Satan, America, has stolen from you what is rightfully yours. Come join the army of Allah in our jihad to conquer the West."

Many Muslims realize, however, that their poverty is the result of backward policies. An unnamed Algerian man once voiced this opinion in an interview: "Algeria was once the granary of Rome, and now it has to import cereals to make bread. It is a land of flocks and gardens, and it imports meat and fruit. It is rich in oil and gas, and it has a foreign debt of $25 billion and two million unemployed."[167]

Third, *the Islamic government appeases angry radicals.* Even if the bureaucracy is filled with mainstream Muslims, they still fear the Islamist hardliners. Have you ever wondered why mainstream Muslims never speak out against Muslim extremists? You might think that all Muslims simply agree with the Islamists and terrorists—but that's not true. Many Muslims would like to speak out—but they don't dare. They fear that if they do, the extremists will target *them.*

Appeasement is the policy of most Middle East governments. Let me give you an example:

A number of years ago, radical Islamists seized a church in the town of Basateen, near Cairo, and turned it into a mosque. The Christians complained to the authorities that the Muslims had stolen their property. What did the police do? They demolished the building, claiming the church lacked the required permits.

Instead of confronting the Muslim militants, the police took the easy way out. The Islamists didn't mind losing their new mosque as long as it meant that the Christians had no church. This kind of appeasement of radical Islamists happens all the time.

BLOOD IN THE WATER

In February 2015, the Salafi jihadist group ISIS released a graphic five-minute video titled *A Message Signed with Blood to the Nations of the Cross* that showed the beheading of twenty-one Coptic Christian men. The terrorists had kidnapped the men—all construction workers—from Sirte, Libya, and took them to a beach on the Mediterranean Sea. All but one of the men were Egyptian.

Before their execution, the men called upon Jesus. The single non-Egyptian man, Mathew Ayairga from West Africa, was not a Christian when he was kidnapped, but when he saw the courage of his Christian companions, he gave his life to Christ. The terrorists offered to let him live if he would renounce Christ, but he said, "Their God is my God."[168]

After the beheadings, the hooded ISIS spokesman pointed his knife to the sea, toward Rome, and said, "We will conquer Rome by Allah's permission."[169]

After the video was released, the U.S. State Department pretended not to know the terrorists' motives, referring to the twenty-one men not as martyred Christians but simply as "Egyptian citizens." Political science professor Daniel Philpott of Notre Dame criticized the Obama administration for refusing to name the real reason for ISIS's bloody act: Islamist anti-Christian hate.[170]

The video made the terrorists' message unmistakably clear: ISIS spilled Christian blood into the sea so that it might flow toward the Vatican in Rome. The beheadings were thus a declaration of war against all of Christendom.

They are inspired and motivated by the ancient prophecies, such as this one from the Sunni hadith: "[Armies carrying] black flags will come from Khurasaan [Iran and Afghanistan]. No power will be able to stop them and they will finally reach Eela [Baitul Maqdas, the Al-Aqsa Mosque in Jerusalem] where they will erect their flags."[171]

A COORDINATED EFFORT TO DEFLECT CRITICISM

In February 2025, a man drove a car into a crowd of striking workers in Munich, Germany, killing a mother and her two-year-old daughter, and injuring more than thirty others. The driver was a twenty-four-year-old man from Afghanistan who had arrived in Germany in 2017 as an unaccompanied minor.

When the police arrested the driver, he shouted, "Allahu akbar!" The young man's social media account, it turned out, was loaded with radical Islamist propaganda. The police concluded—reluctantly, it seemed—that the incident was "most likely" motivated by Islamist ideology. In a tragically ironic twist, the mother and toddler who were killed were Muslim immigrants from Algeria.

The striking workers were all members of Verdi, a far-left European socialist union.[172] Immediately after the attack, the leaders of the union issued a statement downplaying the murderous event as a "token strike" and warned against any "misplaced passion," and called for continued "solidarity and togetherness."[173]

In other words, these leftist leaders didn't want any union members to blame Islamists for this attack—a reminder that the leftists, Progressives, Socialists, and Islamists are all part of one big Red-Green Alliance, the Omnicause, and no one is allowed to break ranks and tell the truth about a terrorist attack in Munich.

The German government also downplayed the attack. As German journalist Sabine Beppler-Spahl observed, "The public's distrust of the government on migration issues isn't hard to comprehend. The reactions to this latest attack have followed a predictable and revealing pattern: despite expressions of shock after each incident, there's always a coordinated effort from establishment voices to control the public narrative and deflect criticism of migration policies. Their primary concern appears to be containing populist pressure rather than honestly and seriously addressing the underlying issues that fuel it."[174]

The German government, like most European governments, will not admit that its policies of lax borders and permissive immigration have let in an unknown number of dangerous Islamists—radicals who are bent on killing Westerners and overthrowing Western society. Instead, these governments silence anyone who speaks the truth.

JIHAD BY MIGRATION

Why are only Western countries expected to take in refugees? Why aren't Arab countries welcoming fellow Arabs? Doesn't it make more sense to send Muslim refugees to Muslim countries than to send them to a strange, non-Islamic culture in Europe?

Part of the answer is that nations such as Saudi Arabia, Qatar, Kuwait, the United Arab Emirates, and Oman are major sponsors of the expansionist Wahhabi-Salafi school of Islam, and sending radicalized "asylum seekers" into the West is part of their deliberate strategy.

The Islamic tradition of *hijrah* (migration) goes back to AD 622, when Muhammad led his followers from Mecca to Yathrib (now Medina) and thus transformed him into a political and military leader. Today, *hijrah* remains a key strategy for Islamic expansion into other lands.

The Quran says that migrating in order to spread Islam is an act of self-sacrifice that Allah will reward: "Whoso migrateth for the cause of Allah will find much refuge and abundance in the earth, and whoso forsaketh his home, a fugitive unto Allah and His messenger, and death overtaketh him, his reward is then incumbent on Allah. Allah is ever Forgiving, Merciful" (Quran 4:100).[175]

Years ago, ISIS published a troubling document called *Libya: The Strategic Gateway for the Islamic State.* The Quilliam Foundation (a British counter-extremism think tank that ceased operation in 2021) translated and analyzed the document, and found it to be a strategic plan to use Libya as a way station for sending jihadists into Europe disguised as refugees. The document pointed out that Libya, just 300 miles from Europe, was well supplied with weapons. Libya's long coastline, the document stated, "looks upon the southern Crusader states, which can be reached with ease by even a rudimentary boat."[176] Thousands of refugees have reached Europe by exactly that route.

In September 2015, Sheikh Muhammad Ayed addressed a Muslim audience at Jerusalem's Al-Aqsa Mosque. He said, "Throughout Europe, all the hearts are infused with hatred toward Muslims. They wish that we were dead. But they have lost their fertility, so they look for fertility in their midst. We will give them fertility! We will breed children with them, because we shall conquer their countries—whether you like it or not, O Germans, O Americans,

O French, O Italians, and all those like you. Take the refugees! We shall soon collect them in the name of the coming Caliphate."[177]

Western audiences were never supposed to hear Sheikh Ayed's words, but thanks to the translators of the Middle East Media Research Institute (MEMRI), we can hear the Islamists themselves proclaim their goals.

Why are so many Muslim immigrants moving to the West? In 2011, the transnational liberation movement known as the Arab Spring swept across the Middle East and North Africa. This movement began as a wave of hope for millions of people living under cruel, authoritarian regimes, but soon disintegrated as shockwaves of riots and civil wars produced a new resurgence of oppressive dictatorships.

The poverty, starvation, and political repression that spread in the wake of the failed Arab Spring movement sent millions of people known as "asylum seekers" flooding into other nations, including Europe and America. But along with those genuine asylum seekers came many Islamists who were not searching for freedom and a better way of life, but were carrying out *hijrah*, or jihad by migration.

When Western governments allow huge numbers of unvetted Muslims across their borders, they are effectively importing jihad to their lands.

A THREE-PRONGED STRATEGY

Focused on global conquest, Islamists seek to overpower the Christian West through a three-pronged strategy: (1) a program of intimidation, from threats of labeling opponents "Islamophobes" to threats of violence and terrorism; (2) the use of the vast oil wealth of the Middle East to bribe, blackmail, and manipulate Western governments and institutions; and (3) changing the demographics of the West through migration and having many children. The strategy is working.

European Muslims have an average of one more child per woman than non-Muslim Europeans (2.6 children per Muslim woman versus 1.6 per non-Muslim woman). In the United Kingdom and France, Muslim women average 2.9 children per woman versus 1.9 for non-Muslims. In the United States, Muslim women have an average of 2.4 children, while the overall American average is 2.1 children per woman, according to Pew Research.[178]

The Third Jihad is well underway. Because of misplaced notions of "tolerance" or "compassion" or "political correctness," or simply out of a greedy desire to import cheap labor, many Western countries have thrown open their gates to an Islamic invasion.

Does this mean the jihadists are destined to conquer the West? No. It's not too late—not yet. But Western civilization is well on its way to destroying itself from within.

Unless we repent as a culture, *our own foolishness* will destroy the civilization it has taken centuries to build. The Islamists will simply walk in and take it over—and our children and grandchildren will pay the price for our folly.

In Abraham Lincoln's Lyceum Address, delivered more than two decades before he became president, he warned that the only way America could be destroyed is if we destroy it ourselves from within. He said, "Shall we expect some transatlantic military giant to step the ocean and crush us at a blow? Never! All the armies of Europe, Asia, and Africa combined . . . could not by force take a drink from the Ohio or make a track on the Blue Ridge in a trial of a thousand years. . . . If destruction be our lot, we must ourselves be its author and finisher. As a nation of free men, we must live through all time or die by suicide.[179]

Will America and the West die by suicide? This generation—you and me—are the only ones who can answer that question. Western civilization can only be conquered by radical Islam if it is first hollowed out from within.

9

ARE WE COMMITTING CULTURAL SUICIDE?

In 1546, after the Church of England broke from the Roman Catholic Church, Parliament bestowed the title "Defender of the Faith" on King Henry VIII and on all future British monarchs. Today, "Defender of the Faith" is one of the titles of King Charles III, along with "Supreme Governor of the Church of England."

But in 1994, nearly three decades before becoming king, Charles, the Prince of Wales, announced that he didn't see himself as "Defender of *the* Faith." Rather, he preferred the title "Defender of *Faith*," the defender of religious faith in general, not the Christian faith in particular. He reaffirmed his dislike of the title "Defender of the Faith" in a combative 2005 conversation with George Carey, the Archbishop of Canterbury.[180]

As Tim Black of the current-events journal *Spiked* observed, King Charles "is an unabashed Islamophile. . . . There is definitely one faith that he prefers above all others. And it's not that of the Church of England."[181]

King Charles' admiration for Islam has been well known for years. In 1996, Nazim al-Haqqani, the grand mufti of Cyprus, announced that then-Prince Charles was a closet Muslim. "Did you know that Prince Charles has converted to Islam?" Al-Haqqani said. "Yes, yes. He is a Muslim. I can't say more."[182]

The official response from Buckingham Palace: "Nonsense."[183]

I don't think King Charles III is a Muslim—but it's easy to understand why the late grand mufti thought so.

COMPROMISED JUDGMENT

As prince, Charles studied Arabic with a private tutor so that he could read the Quran in the original language.[184] He expressed his love for the Quran by creating the Carpet Garden at his Highgrove House residence, the garden's layout inspired by two Turkish carpets in the house.[185] He said, "I planted fig, pomegranate, and olive trees in the garden because of their mention in the Quran."[186]

King Charles' admiration for Islam has earned him many friends in the Muslim world. Some of those friendships, however, seem to have compromised his judgment.

In 2022, *The Sunday Times* revealed that, on three occasions from 2011 to 2015, Prince Charles personally accepted cash-filled luggage from a Qatari official as donations to the prince's charitable fund. Each gift consisted of a million euros in the form of €500 notes—the so-called "bin Laden denomination" often used to finance terrorism. Much of the money was packed into handbags from Fortnum & Mason, London's snobbiest luxury store. An aide who handled the cash said, "Everyone felt very uncomfortable about the situation."

The Qatari donor was Sheikh Hamad bin Jassim bin Jaber Al Thani (nicknamed "HBJ"), who was Qatar's prime minister from 2007 to 2013. There's no hint that Charles did anything illegal in accepting the charitable donation, but the more we know about the Qatari donor, the more we have to question Charles' judgment.

Sheikh Hamad bin Jassim, one of the richest men in the world, was the original owner of the "Palace in the Sky," the $400-million luxury jet that Qatar gifted to President Donald Trump in 2025. He was prime minister during the years when Qatar gave around two billion dollars to support the Palestinian terror group Hamas.

The *Times* also reported that HBJ gave Prince Charles "a £147,000 horse named Dark Swan" and contributed to maintaining a castle in Scotland owned by Charles. These gifts are legal but, as the

Times concludes, they raise questions about Charles' "impartiality in representing Britain on the world stage."[187]

"GROSSLY DISTORTED" JUDGMENT

For decades, King Charles actively championed Islam as more enlightened than Western civilization and more enlightened than Christianity. In October 1993, the then Prince of Wales became the patron of the Oxford Centre for Islamic Studies and delivered a lecture called "Islam and the West."

"Our judgment of Islam has been grossly distorted," he told the audience. Westerners, he claimed, are guilty of "unthinking prejudices" against Sharia law. "My own understanding is that extremes, like the cutting off of hands, are rarely practiced. The guiding principle and spirit of Islamic law . . . [are] those of equity and compassion."[188]

Charles' rose-tinted description of Sharia law—a system that includes *hudud* punishments (amputations, lashings, stonings), severe restrictions on women's rights, and a death penalty for converting to another religion—makes us wonder: *Whose* judgment is "grossly distorted"?

Terrorism, Prince Charles claimed, has nothing to do with Islamic ideology. It is simply the result of "extremism." He explained, "Extremism is no more the monopoly of Islam than it is the monopoly of other religions, including Christianity."[189] If that's so, where are the Episcopalian suicide bombers?

Charles went on to claim, "The Prophet himself always disliked and feared extremism."[190] Was he unaware of the famous Sword Verse, Quran 9:5, which commands, "Slay the idolaters wherever ye find them"? Or other Quranic commands to slaughter, such as Quran 2:191 and 8:12? These texts seem extremist to me.

First as prince, and now as king, Charles III projects onto Islam what he wants it to be, not what it really is. For decades, he has been whitewashing Islam while disparaging his own culture as bigoted and backward. Patrick Sookhdeo, director of the Institute for the Study of Islam and Christianity, notes that Charles unfairly compares "the best ideals of the Islamic faith with the worst of Western cultural decadence."

King Charles seems unaware that the Muslim world is like a puddle of gasoline next to an open flame—and its volatility is due to the warlike doctrines of the Quran. Both the Muslim world and the Western world desperately need to be reformed by values of freedom, respect for individual rights, and respect for truth. These are distinctly Christian values—and the Defender of the Faith should know that.

THE HERESIES THAT INFLUENCED MUHAMMAD

We can't count on King Charles to defend the Christian faith, but God has called on you and me to be defenders of the faith. As the apostle Peter reminds us, "In your hearts revere Christ as Lord. Always be prepared to give an answer to everyone who asks you to give the reason for the hope that you have. But do this with gentleness and respect" (1 Peter 3:15).

And as Jesus himself said in the Book of Revelation, "Hold on to what you have until I come" (Revelation 2:25).

I don't fear the jihadists and terrorists nearly as much as I fear that the Christian Church might depart from the Scriptures. Militant Islam always grows stronger when Christianity weakens—and it retreats when Christians stand firm on the truth of God's Word.

In its early years, the Muslim religion fed on the remains of a Christian Church that had become sickened with heresies and apostasy. As a result, alongside the true "wheat" of faithful Christian churches, the "weeds" of false religions sprang up, just as Jesus predicted in Matthew 13:24–30. The Christian world was riddled with breakaway cults such as Arianism (which taught that Christ was a subordinate being, not co-equal with God the Father), Nestorianism (which split the deity of Christ from his humanity), and Sabellianism (which denied the Trinity). Two cults in particular—the Docetics and the Ebionites—probably influenced Muhammad's thinking.

The Docetics believed that Jesus only appeared to be human and that his crucifixion was an illusion, while the Ebionites viewed Jesus as a human prophet and the Messiah but denied that he was the Son of God. They were legalists who adhered strictly to Jewish law. The legalism of Islam and the Quran's false portrayal of Jesus are thus probably rooted in the practices and false doctrines of the cults of that era.

The Arabian Peninsula was especially vulnerable to false religious ideas. The Arab people practiced a form of idolatry that mingled pagan idolatry with various strands of Judaism and assorted ideas from pseudo-Christian cults. In fact, when true Christian missionaries came to evangelize the pre-Islamic Arabs, the Arabs said, "We've already heard about Jesus. We're not interested in your gospel."

Perhaps if the true Christian gospel of salvation by grace through faith in Christ had reached Muhammad's ears, he might have been a great evangelist, an Arabian apostle Paul. Instead, he founded a religion that has become Christendom's fiercest foe.

Nevertheless, Muhammad's view of Christianity was undoubtedly influenced by false believers and their heresies. The Church in North Africa had once been strong and faithful to God's Word, producing such revered church fathers as Cyprian of Carthage and Augustine of Hippo, but by the fifth century, it was permeated with false doctrines, and many churches had fallen away from the faith.

From 647 to 648, Muslim armies under Umar, the second caliph, marched across Egypt and into Libya. Many Christians were so biblically uninformed that they actually welcomed Islamic teachings into the Church as a new revelation, with many weak Christians allowing their churches to be converted into mosques without putting up a fight.

A second wave of Islamic conquest rolled across North Africa from 665 to 689, wresting control of the region from the decaying, nominally Christian Byzantine Empire. A third wave of conquest, from the early 690s to 709, gave the Islamic caliphate control of North Africa, and the Church in North Africa effectively ceased to exist.

HERESIES THAT AFFLICT US TODAY

Although the pseudo-Christian cults of Muhammad's time are gone, Western Christianity is threatened by a new array of heresies, including:

- *Universalism*: This movement claims that all people will ultimately receive salvation, regardless of what they believe and the way they live their lives. These beliefs are found in both Christian Universalism and Unitarian Universalism.
- *Progressive Christianity*: This movement is focused on social justice and preaching a "social gospel" that has more to do with Progressive politics than with the teachings of Jesus.
- *Post-Evangelicalism*: People who have discarded biblical faith due to changing their theological, political, or cultural views often describe themselves as Post-Evangelicals.
- *The Emerging Church*: This is an organized faction of false teachers within Christianity who want to "deconstruct" and "reconstruct" what it means to be a "Christian" in our postmodern culture. It leads its followers toward worldly thinking—and often ends up causing churches to split or dissolve.
- *The Insider Movement*: A religious movement in which converts to Christianity, usually from Muslim or Hindu cultures, remain within their existing religious and cultural communities while identifying (usually secretly) as followers of Jesus Christ. The result, all too often, is that those secret Christians are inexorably pressured to conform to the false teaching that surrounds them.
- *Hyper-Grace*: This is an updated version of the ancient false teaching known as Antinomianism—the notion that moral laws don't apply to Christians under grace. This view leads to a disregard for biblical ethics and morality. Hyper-Grace rejects the idea that Jesus must be Lord as well as Savior.
- *Chrislam*: This is a modern-day effort to blend the doctrines and practices of Christianity and Islam. The Chrislam movement originated in Nigeria during the 1970s as an attempt to ease tensions between Christians and Muslims, with early Chrislamists

trying to unite the two faiths by focusing on what they have in common while downplaying their differences.

The faith we defend is a set of bedrock truths: Jesus is God incarnate, the sacrifice for our sin, the only begotten Son of the Father, full of grace and truth. That is the heart of Christianity. If you take the heart out of the body, you are left with a corpse.

The "Christianity" that Muhammad saw was a corpse without a beating heart of truth. No wonder he reacted against it. And no wonder that Islam, the religion Muhammad founded, is now the sworn enemy of the Christian faith.

Today, Christianity is again riddled with heresies and weakened by false teachings, with many churches and individual Christians falling away from true faith. They are creating the same spiritual vacuum that Islam was so quick to fill in the 7th century. In the 21st century, Islam is again poised to fill the spiritual vacuum left by the decline of Christianity.

But it's not too late to rededicate ourselves to defending the faith. It's not too late to prevent Western civilization from committing cultural suicide.

TAXPAYERS ARE FUNDING JIHAD

The Islamists have been declaring their intentions for decades, and our response has been to simply close our eyes and cover our ears and pretend the Islamists don't mean what they say. We keep subsidizing the jihadists as they wage war against us.

A March 2009 incident in Luton, northwest of London, should have been a ten-alarm warning to us all. At that time, Great Britain was involved in the Iraq War, which began in 2003, and the 2nd Battalion Royal Anglian Regiment was returning to Luton after completing a second tour in Iraq. As the soldiers marched down the street, thousands of cheering people turned out for the homecoming.

But among the welcoming crowd was a small group of Islamists who shouted, "Rapists! Murderers! Cowards! Baby killers!" The Islamist activists, along with their leader, Anjem Choudary, were arrested and charged with offenses against the public order, including making threats.

During their trial in January 2010, the Islamists showed contempt for the court by refusing to stand when the judge entered the courtroom (the judge could have charged them with contempt but said she did not want to "set a precedent" by doing so).

Incredibly, the Islamists claimed in court that their words were not intended to "upset" anyone. In fact, Choudary claimed that it was "impossible" that the soldiers or their supporters would have been offended because the protesters were merely speaking the truth.

The defendants were treated with an extra measure of respect. The court gave them an extended lunch hour so they could pray at a nearby mosque, and a "quiet room" for prayers was set aside for them in the courthouse.

During the six-day trial, supporters of the defendants stood outside the courthouse, holding signs that declared, "Islam Will Dominate the World! Freedom Can Go to Hell!" (Although perhaps hard to believe, Islamist hardliners really do hate freedom. They believe that Allah has spoken through Muhammad, that his revelation in the Quran is final and absolute, and freedom can only lead people into error and sin. What the world needs, they believe, is absolute, universal submission to Allah, not freedom.)

The defendants were found guilty but received conditional discharges—no punishment as long as they do not reoffend. Though the offense carries a maximum fine of £1,000, they were only required to pay £500 in court costs.

Outside the court, the Islamists bragged that they all received welfare benefits from the British taxpayers. "The taxpayer paid for this court case," they said. "The taxpayer will pay for the fines too out of benefits."[191]

In fact, Anjem Choudary has made a video that is widely circulated among Islamists in Great Britain, showing them how to collect Britain's generous Jobseeker's Allowance. This way, the Islamists could support their families, fund a "Muslim holy war" against the West, and never have to work a single day. British taxpayers are thus funding the jihad waged against them.[192] As Choudary himself said, "I am not on Jobseeker's Allowance. I'm on jihad seeker's allowance."[193]

The Islamist defendants told reporters that being fined is a "medal of honor," and that the conviction would not deter them from future protests. "This case," one of them said, "shows the need for Sharia law. British law is not credible."[194]

HOW ISLAMISTS ARE RECRUITED

The story of Anjem Choudary—the leader of the protesters in Luton—demonstrates how hard it is to root out radical Islamism in a free society. The Islamists have become skilled at using Western laws and Western freedoms against us.

According to BBC home affairs correspondent Dominic Casciani, "Anjem Choudary could probably have been anything he wanted to be." He began his university career as a medical student, then switched to the study of law and passed the exams to qualify as a solicitor (similar to an attorney in the U.S.). He worked largely on anti-discrimination cases, advocating for fellow Muslims.

In his student days, Choudary liked to drink and party—until a Syrian-born Islamic cleric with ties to Al-Qaeda recruited him into the world of Islamist activism. The cleric, Omar Bakri Muhammad, mentored Choudary and inspired him to believe in a future global caliphate under the absolute rule of Sharia law. Dominic Casciani observed that, after Anjem Choudary was radicalized, he became "one of the most dangerous men in Britain."

How was he dangerous? He didn't set off bombs or shoot people or hijack airplanes. But for two decades, he was a preacher who inspired *other* people to commit acts of violence. He was, wrote Casciani, "an ideologue, a thinker, who encouraged others not to stop and think for themselves before they turned to violence to implement their shared worldview."

Choudary offered his disciples a simple way of looking at the world—the world of the believers (Muslims) versus the rest of the world (the unbelievers). For young men who found the world complex and confusing, Choudary offered black-and-white simplicity.

He also offered his disciples a utopian goal to believe in: a worldwide Islamic state.

One of Choudary's disciples (who later became disillusioned) was Adam Deen, who told the BBC, "What attracted me was the simplicity, that I was a Muslim, that . . . I belonged inside an Islamic state and everything else was wrong and evil. . . . It's a type of outlook that is completely splitting the world in a cosmic battle of good and evil. And on the side of good is everyone who agrees with what he says. That polarization creates a type of mindset towards non-Muslims—and then you can start rationalizing acts of violence."

Choudary was, however, too clever to commit crimes himself. He promised his followers that "the flag of Islam will fly over Downing Street" (the residence of the British prime minister) and filled their minds with Islamist ideology and hate—then let them take all the risks.

One of his followers, Omar Sharif, blew himself up in a suicide bombing in Tel Aviv. Another, Brusthom Ziamani, was sentenced to a dozen years in prison for planning a terror attack in London. One of his closest followers, Michael Adebolajo, got in a car with an accomplice and ran down a twenty-five-year-old off-duty British soldier. The two men then jumped out of the car and stabbed and hacked the soldier to death. Then they stood over the body of the murdered man, Lee James Rigby of the Royal Regiment of Fusiliers, and told passers-by that they had murdered him as an act of jihad. Both were captured and now serve life sentences.

But Choudary, who had inspired all these crimes with his rhetoric, left no fingerprints and couldn't be caught—until 2015. That's when Scotland Yard investigated his recruitment activities and found that he had been urging young Muslims to join ISIS—in violation of Britain's Terrorism Act 2000. Choudary was imprisoned for five and a half years, and required to notify police of any change of address for the next fifteen years. At his sentencing, his supporters in the gallery shouted, "Allahu Akbar!"[195]

All across the Western world, there are people like Anjem Choudary—people who know how to use our laws and our freedom against us. Our secular left and Progressive leaders in America and

Europe have opened the floodgates of rampant immigration, allowing not only needy asylum seekers but dangerous, ideologically driven Islamists into our midst. These leftist leaders are giving away our rights, our safety, and our civilization. They are taking us down the path of cultural suicide.

IS IT TOO LATE?

A few Western voices have, however, begun to sound the alarm. Former NBC television correspondent David Ben-Basat warned in an opinion piece, "What's unfolding in the UK should raise red flags across Europe. The political Islam creeping into decision-making centers through democratic votes represents a dangerous intersection of liberty and vulnerability. . . . Britain, once a global leader in civil liberties and the fight against fascism, now faces a new test: a test of identity. The lingering question is whether the country will regain its footing—or whether, within less than three decades, ethnic Britons will become a minority in their own homeland."[196]

Christopher Caldwell, senior fellow at the Claremont Institute, agrees. He warned, "Europe imported a minority with a radical identity. . . . In doing so, it forfeited its own identity and culture."[197]

Hugh Fitzgerald, author of *Islamizing Europe: Is the Conquest Inevitable?*, writes, "More than four million Muslims, both migrants and native-born, now live in Britain. . . . Muslims in Britain vote as a bloc. . . . They are being elected to local councils, becoming mayors (think of Sadiq Khan, mayor of London), and members of Parliament. As their numbers inexorably rise, due to continued immigration, legal and illegal, and to disparate fertility rates, so will their political power. Political Islam is on the march."[198]

What will be the impact of increasing Islamic political power in the UK and other Western nations? Fitzgerald warns of Muslim political demands for more anti-Israel policies, more Muslim immigration, more "no-go" areas where non-Muslims and even police fear to tread, more wealth transferred from taxpayers to Islamist welfare recipients, more Sharia courts and Sharia influence, and more rewriting of history in textbooks to favor Islam and disparage the West.

In fact, Fitzgerald observes that these dire effects could happen before we know it. "It will not be necessary for Muslims to be a majority to have such an influence," he writes. "In countries where Muslims are 20 to 30 percent of the population, their cohesion has allowed them to wield great power. Those numbers could be attained by 2040, but only if nothing is done to halt Muslim immigration and to increase deportation, beginning with all those migrants, overwhelmingly Muslims, who have been convicted of crimes."[199]

For many middle-class Britons, there's a growing sense that they are losing their culture—and their children's lives are at risk. The frustration of British parents reached full boil after July 29, 2024, when seventeen-year-old Axel Rudakubana went on a stabbing rampage at a children's party in Southport, England. Rudakubana, a British-born Muslim and the son of Rwandan immigrants, murdered three little girls, ages six, seven, and nine, and left six other children and two adults critically wounded and traumatized for life. Police later found an Al-Qaeda manual among the killer's possessions. News of the attack triggered protests across England and Northern Ireland.

In June 2025, a thirty-eight-year-old Ethiopian man named Hadush Kebatu reached the southeast shore of England by boat and claimed asylum in the United Kingdom. The British government took him to the Bell Hotel in Epping, where, over the objections of the townspeople and the town council, the government was housing male asylum seekers.

Kebatu had only been on British soil for seven days before he approached a fourteen-year-old girl in an Epping restaurant and forcibly tried to kiss her. He made similar approaches to other Epping girls. He was arrested and charged with sexual assault and enticing a minor to engage in sexual activity.

Soon after Kebatu's arrest, more than a thousand townspeople gathered at the hotel, chanting, "Save our kids!" It was a spontaneous outpouring of fury directed at a government that placed leftist ideology ahead of children's safety. Within days, the town council voted unanimously to petition the Home Office to remove the asylum seekers from Epping.

Far-left activists and agitators from Stand Up to Racism and the Socialist Workers Party quickly mobilized, swarming into Epping to confront the townspeople. Incredibly, the police sided with the leftist activists and against the local people of Epping, with the confrontation turning into a full-blown riot—and police only arrested local men.

Dominic Green of The Free Press wrote, "Social media carried footage of police escorting the far-left outsiders to meet the local protesters, and using dogs and nightsticks against the locals. . . . Epping is now the frontline of Britain's migrant crisis and the even more profound crisis of trust between a government and its people."[200]

Though national media outlets ignored the story, news of the parents' uprising in Epping spread on social media, with protests breaking out against asylum hotels in more than twenty cities across England and Scotland. Britain's prime minister, Keir Starmer (who calls himself a "socialist" and a "progressive"[201]), demanded that the Epping townspeople be given "exemplary sentencing," and claimed that the grassroots protests were "coordinated" by the "far right."

When Dominic Green interviewed the townspeople of Epping, he found them to be not at all as Keir Starmer described them. Green found one interviewee, a woman by the name of Kelly, to be a person of genuine compassion for refugees. Those who "truly need help," she said, should be welcome. But the asylum seekers in Epping, she said, shouldn't be receiving British welfare, because they had already passed through a number of "safe countries" to get to Britain.

It's true. As Dominic Green reports, asylum seekers often travel through a number of European countries on their way to Great Britain, but criminal gangs of smugglers advertise in Africa, the Middle East, and South Asia that Britain offers generous welfare benefits. In fact, the gangs get rich smuggling Muslims to Britain—and the taxpayers then get stuck with the bill.

Just as the Biden administration flung open the southern border of the United States for four years, the Labour government of Keir Starmer does nothing to prevent boats filled with asylum seekers—overwhelmingly Muslim men—from crossing the English Channel.

Once they arrive, the Home Office buses them to communities across Great Britain.

One Epping woman told Dominic Green, "I think this country is gone. There's no saving it now."[202]

I understand why this woman has lost hope. But, as desperate as the situation may seem, many people in Great Britain, Europe, and America are rising up and demanding protection for their children, protection for their communities, and protection for their civilization. They are calling on their leaders do the job they were elected to do. They demand that Western law be enforced to protect children and society from those who seek to impose Sharia law on us all.

As long as people of good conscience have the courage to make their voices heard, there is still hope to save our civilization from cultural suicide.

10

ISLAM, THE END TIMES, AND THE ANTICHRIST

In 2014, the Salafi jihadist organization that calls itself "the Islamic State" (also known as ISIS or Daesh) declared itself to be the global caliphate, claiming to have religious and political authority over all Muslims throughout the world. Most Muslims rejected this claim, and many Muslim nations, including Saudi Arabia, designated ISIS a terrorist organization.

The year 2014 is also when ISIS began publishing the online magazine *Dabiq*, which it circulated on the "deep web" (websites that are not indexed by search engines). The title of the magazine comes from the town of Dabiq in northern Syria.

At that time, the jihadists of ISIS were at the peak of their strength, winning victory after victory across Iraq and Syria and believing they were fulfilling a prophecy contained in the Hadith: "The Last Hour would not come until the Romans land at Al-A'maq or in Dabiq. An army consisting of the best (soldiers) of the people of the earth at that time will come from Medina (to counteract them)."[203]

According to this Islamic prophecy, the armies of Islam will fight and defeat the armies of the "Romans" (that is, Europeans or Christians) at Dabiq. This will take place during the *Malahim* (the time of fierce wars) leading up to the *Yawm ad-Din* (the Day of Judgment). The ISIS fighters thus believed they were in the midst of the time of fierce wars, and they were bringing the world closer to the Day of Judgment.

ISIS also used their magazine *Dabiq* as a recruitment tool to attract Muslims from around the world to join the caliphate and fight their way to the town of Dabiq for the long-prophesied battle. The magazine published full-color photos of gruesome atrocities the ISIS fighters committed, plus articles promising to reinstitute ancient Islamic practices, such as the sex enslavement of non-Muslim women.[204]

In August 2014, ISIS conquered the town of Dabiq, killing many Syrians and destroying ancient shrines, and holding the town for more than two years. The fighters were convinced that the "Romans" could come at any time to trigger the battle predicted by the Hadith.

Then, in the fall of 2016, a joint operation of the Turkish army and the Free Syrian Army pushed ISIS out of Dabiq. The surviving ISIS fighters were stunned to discover they had not fulfilled the prophecy after all.[205] *Dabiq* ceased publication soon after, and for the next three years, ISIS suffered defeat after defeat as its caliphate steadily shrunk.

In March 2019, the global coalition liberated the last remaining ISIS stronghold in Baghouz in eastern Syria, and so ISIS was territorially defeated, losing all the land it had once controlled in Iraq and Syria. The self-declared caliphate ceased to exist. In October 2019, ISIS leader Abu Bakr al-Baghdadi was killed by the U.S. military.[206]

The prophecies in the Quran and the Hadith will never be fulfilled. They can't be, because they contradict the prophecies of the Bible. As Christians, however, we know that many prophecies in the Old Testament have already been fulfilled. The birth of Jesus in Bethlehem (Micah 5:2), his suffering and death on the cross (Isaiah 53 and Psalm 22), his resurrection (Psalm 16:10), and even the 1948 reestablishment of the State of Israel (Ezekiel 36–37 and Isaiah 66:8) are all fulfillments of Old Testament prophecies.

There are no biblical prophecies that specifically mention Islam, yet it seems certain that the Muslim world has an important role to play in God's plan for the End Times. In fact, it's hard to imagine how the cataclysmic future events predicted in Daniel, Matthew, and Revelation could take place without involving the Islamic nations that encircle Israel. Let's explore the role that biblical prophecy seems to outline for the people of the Muslim world.

STARTLING PARALLELS

Bible interpreters have a range of views on Bible prophecy in general and the Great Tribulation in particular. Differences in viewpoints focus on when the Rapture will occur—that is, when Jesus will return to gather his Church and take believers to Heaven. Pre-tribulationists believe the Church will be raptured (taken to Heaven) before the Great Tribulation begins. Mid-tribulationists hold that the Church will be raptured in the middle of the seven-year Tribulation. Post-tribulationists believe the Church will endure the Tribulation and be raptured at the Second Coming of Christ.

On this subject, I'm a "pan-tribulationist." I'm waiting to see how the future "pans out."

Some Bible interpreters believe that the Antichrist will be revealed at the start of the Tribulation, probably through the confirmation of a seven-year covenant that Daniel describes in Daniel 9:27. Others believe the Antichrist will not be easy for the world to recognize until the mid-point of the Tribulation, when he breaks the covenant with Israel, sets up the "abomination of desolation" in the temple in Jerusalem, and demands the worship of the world.

I tend to think that many Muslims will receive the Antichrist as their Mahdi and throw their support behind him. This could happen at the beginning of the Tribulation, or at the mid-point of the Tribulation, when the Antichrist breaks his covenant with Israel.

Whatever view of the Tribulation you hold, I believe we can all agree on one underlying principle: We are united in watching and waiting for the Lord's return, and in living faithfully and obediently until he comes.

All three Abrahamic religions devote a great deal of attention to eschatology, the study of the prophecies of the End Times.

There are startling parallels between the prophetic teachings of these three religions:

Jerusalem. The eschatological prophecies of all three religions have a major focus on events in and around Jerusalem and the Mount of Olives.

Signs Preceding Judgment. All three religions speak of prophetic signs that point to the approaching End Times Final Judgment. (Jesus speaks of these signs in Matthew 24:4–28.)

The Messiah. All three religions predict the coming of the Messiah.

Judaism teaches that the Messiah will restore the kingdom of Israel and that God will be Israel's King (Zechariah 14).

Christianity teaches that Jesus the Messiah came to earth 2,000 years ago, that he was crucified and resurrected, and that he will return to Earth, defeat the Antichrist, and rule over his messianic kingdom (Matthew 19:28 and Revelation 20:4–6).

Islam teaches that Jesus (whom Muslims call Isa) is a prophet and the Masîḥ (Arabic for "Messiah"), and Muslims thus believe that Isa will return to help the Imam Mahdi defeat the Al-Masih ad-Dajjal (the Islamic Antichrist).

Final War. All three religions predict a cataclysmic global war.

Judaism teaches that, in this ultimate war, the Messiah will lead Israel to victory over its enemies.

Christianity teaches that Satan will instigate the final conflict, which the Bible calls the Battle of Armageddon.

Islam also predicts that an ultimate battle will be fought. As in Judaism and Christianity, Islamic eschatology refers to the nations of Gog and Magog—*Yajuj* and *Majuj* in Quran 18:94–100.

Sheikh Muhammad Hisham Kabbani, a Sufi scholar, observed, "Jews are waiting for the Messiah, Christians are waiting for Jesus, and Muslims are waiting for both the Mahdi and Jesus. All religions describe them as men coming to save the world."[207]

STRIKING DIFFERENCES

Though there are similarities between the eschatologies of these three religions, the differences between them are even more striking.

The central figure of Islamic eschatology is the Imam Mahdi (*Mahdi* means "the Rightly Guided One"). To Muslims, the Imam Mahdi is the coming savior who will establish the global empire—the ultimate caliphate—and will rule the entire Earth as the rightful successor to Muhammad.

Sunni Muslims and Shia Muslims differ sharply, however, in their views of the Mahdi. Sunnis see the Mahdi as a righteous, wise, and divinely inspired human man but not a supernatural being. They believe he will be born, live a natural life span, and die like any other man.

The largest sect of Shia Muslims—the Twelver Shia sect discussed in chapters 1 and 6—takes a more mystical view of the Mahdi. They believe the Mahdi was a historical figure named Muhammad ibn Hasan al-Mahdī, who was born in 869, became an imam (religious leader) at age five, and is still alive today, more than eleven centuries later. They believe Al-Mahdī underwent "occultation" (being miraculously hidden from the world). He will remain in occultation until he returns to lead the faithful and punish the infidels just before the Day of Judgment.

Roughly one out of ten Muslims are Shias; the rest are overwhelmingly Sunnis. Most Shias live in Iran, Iraq, Azerbaijan, and Bahrain. Being a minority sect within Islam, Shias see themselves as a faithful but persecuted remnant within Islam.

In *The Last Trumpet: A Comparative Study in Christian-Islamic Eschatology*, the late Dr. Shahid—professor of missions in the Islamic Studies program at Southwestern Baptist Theological Seminary—described the Shia view of the mystical Mahdi:

> The Shiites believe that when the Mahdi reappears from his great occultation, he will recover the original book of Psalms from the lake of Tiberius, the Torah and the Gospel, the Ark of the Covenant, the Tablets of Moses and his Staff, and the Ring of Solomon, from a cave in Antioch. . . . The Mahdi will conquer the world and destroy all the infidels . . . [and] take over every city, even Jerusalem, that Alexander the Great vanquished, and [he will] reform them. That will gratify the hearts of the people of Islam. . . .

> The universal Islamic community he establishes is not based on peace or love. It is an earthly militant kingdom under the banner of Islam in which people either will accept the Shiite type of Islam, or will be killed.[208]

You may have already noticed one troubling aspect of Islamic eschatology: Islam's "savior," the Mahdi, bears a striking resemblance *not* to the biblical Christ but to the biblical Antichrist. Why would the Antichrist—Satan's ultimate masterwork—so closely resemble the Mahdi of Islamic eschatology?

I believe it's because Satan—the Deceiver, the Father of Lies—has a thorough understanding of both the Bible and the Quran, and is preparing a grand deception for Muslims. His plan is for Muslims to look upon the Antichrist and see him as their long-prophesied Imam Mahdi—in other words, Satan is preparing the Muslim people to receive the Antichrist as their savior.

THE MAHDI AND THE MASÎḤ

Muslims expect the Mahdi to appear when Jesus (Isa) returns. Though Muslims believe in a prophet named Jesus, they do not accept him as their Savior; nor do they believe he is the Son of God. To Muslims, Jesus is the *Masîḥ* (Messiah), but they deny that he died on the cross.

The person in prophecy whom Muslims most revere is the Mahdi—and his description in Islamic prophecy is almost identical to the Bible's description of the Antichrist. In *Al Mahdi and the End of Time*, Egyptian Islamic scholars Muhammad Ibn Izzat and Muhammad Arif vividly describe the arrival of the Mahdi:

> The Mahdi will be victorious and eradicate those pigs and dogs and the idols of this time so that there will once more be [a] caliphate based on prophethood. . . .
>
> Jerusalem will be the location of the rightly-guided caliphate and the centre of Islamic rule, which will be headed by Imam al-Mahdi. . . .

> That will abolish the leadership of the Jews, who direct the world from within the Masonic circles, and put an end to the domination of the shaytans [satans or demons] who spit evil into people and cause corruption in the earth, making them slaves of false idols and ruling the world by laws other than the Sharia of the Lord of the worlds. It will be the Day of Salvation from this Era of Ignorance.[209]

(Note that these Muslim scholars invoke a common Islamic conspiracy theory, claiming that the Jews are involved with the Freemasons in a secret plot to dominate the world. This conspiracy theory is largely derived from *The Protocols of the Elders of Zion*, a fabricated and discredited document first published in Russia in 1903.)

Izzat and Arif state that "those pigs and dogs" (non-Muslims) will be defeated and eradicated by the Mahdi, and that the Mahdi will replace the Jewish governance of Jerusalem with a "rightly guided" caliphate. The arrival of the Mahdi, these Islamic scholars claim, will usher in the "Day of Salvation." A commonly accepted interpretation of Christian eschatology states that the emergence of the Antichrist will trigger the events of the Tribulation period.

Both the Mahdi and the Antichrist are said to possess supreme political and religious authority, both worshipped as the head of a one-world religion. Like the Antichrist, the Mahdi will establish his capital in Jerusalem, and he will rule the world from that holy city.

The Bible says that the Antichrist will target Jews and Christians for destruction; Islamic eschatology says the Mahdi will wage war against Jews and Christians. Those who oppose the Antichrist will be executed; those who oppose the Mahdi will be executed.

Iranian religious leader Ayatollah Ibrahim Amini writes that the Mahdi "will offer the religion of Islam to the non-believers [Jews, Christians, and other non-Muslims]. Anyone who accepts that call will be saved from being killed. All those who refuse to accept Islam will be killed."[210]

A COVENANT WITH MANY

In Daniel 9:27, we read that the Antichrist "will confirm a covenant with many for one 'seven.' In the middle of the 'seven' he will put an end to sacrifice and offering. And at the temple he will set up an abomination that causes desolation, until the end that is decreed is poured out on him."

So the Antichrist will make a "covenant with many"—a treaty with many nations. Israel will be a signatory of this treaty. Then, "in the middle of the 'seven'"—halfway through the seven-year term of the covenant—the Antichrist will break the covenant. This act of treachery will have catastrophic implications for Israel. The Antichrist will end the temple sacrifices and set up "an abomination that causes desolation" in the temple.

Islam's Hadith also speaks of a seven-year covenant that the Mahdi makes with the "Romans." As one Islamic website explains:

> According to various Islamic theological sources, Al-Mahdi is said to be one who will initiate Islam's fourth and final treaty between the "Romans" and the Muslims. Al-Mahdi will make this treaty for a period of seven years! In a Hadith, Prophet Muhammad (peace be upon him) said: "There will be four peace agreements between you and the Romans. The fourth will be mediated through a person who will be from the progeny of Hazrat Aaron (the brother of Moses) and will be upheld for seven years." The people asked, "O Prophet Muhammad (peace be upon him), who will be the Imam (leader) of the people at that time?" The Prophet said: "He will be from my progeny and will be exactly forty years of age. His face will shine like a star." . . . It appears that the period of this seven-year peace agreement will likewise be the period of the Mahdi's reign.[211]

Let's break this fascinating statement into its component parts and compare the Mahdi of Islam with the Antichrist of the Bible.

First, just as the Antichrist will make a covenant with "many," the Mahdi will make a covenant with the "Romans," or nations of Europe.

Second, both the Mahdi of Islam and the Antichrist of the Bible will make a covenant lasting for seven years.

Third, Islam teaches that the Mahdi will reign during the seven-year term of the peace agreement. The Bible tells us that the Antichrist will reign for seven years.

A TIME OF UNEQUALED DISTRESS

In the Hadith, Abu Sa'id al-Khudri quotes Muhammad as saying, "The Mahdi is of my lineage, with a high forehead and a long, thin, curved nose. He will fill the earth with fairness and justice as it was filled with oppression and injustice, and he will rule for seven years."[212] Here again, we see that the length of the Mahdi's rule is the same as the length of the Antichrist's reign—seven years.

In *Al Mahdi and the End of Time*, Muhammad Ibn Izzat and Muhammad Arif observe that Revelation 6:2 says, "I looked, and there before me was a white horse! Its rider held a bow, and he was given a crown, and he rode out as a conqueror bent on conquest." Most evangelical Bible interpreters believe that the rider on a white horse is a false man of peace, Satan's counterfeit, the Antichrist.

But who do these two Islamic scholars say the rider on the white horse will be? They write, "It is clear that this man is the Mahdi who will ride the white horse and judge by the Quran." In other words, these Islamic scholars *specifically* identify as the Mahdi the man Christians identify as the Antichrist.[213]

When Muslims look forward to a worldwide caliphate, they expect the coming of the Mahdi, the long-prophesied "final Caliph" of Islam. When he appears, all Muslims will be required to give their loyalty to him. Sheikh Muhammad Hisham Kabbani writes that Muhammad said of the Mahdi (in the words of the Hadith narrator Thawban), "If you see him, go and give him your allegiance, even if you have to crawl over ice, because he is the Viceregent [Khalifa] of Allah, the Mahdi."[214]

There can be no doubt. Satan is preparing Muslims to accept the Mahdi as their caliph. And who is the Mahdi? He is unmistakably the Antichrist of the Bible, and when this counterfeit "savior," the Antichrist, arises to impose his iron rule upon the world, Muslims will have been thoroughly prepared to receive him.

The campaign of terrorism that Islamic extremists inflict upon the West is a foretaste of the coming totalitarian reign of the Antichrist. As Jesus foretold, "For then there will be great distress, unequaled from the beginning of the world until now—and never to be equaled again" (Matthew 24:21).

THE COMING FALSE PROPHET

In Revelation 13, John writes about two beasts. He describes the first beast in verses 1 through 4: "The dragon stood on the shore of the sea. And I saw a beast coming out of the sea. It had ten horns and seven heads, with ten crowns on its horns, and on each head a blasphemous name. . . . The dragon gave the beast his power and his throne and great authority. One of the heads of the beast seemed to have had a fatal wound, but the fatal wound had been healed. The whole world was filled with wonder and followed the beast. People worshiped the dragon because he had given authority to the beast, and they also worshiped the beast and asked, 'Who is like the beast? Who can wage war against it?'"

This beast, which came out of the sea and received power from the dragon (Satan), is the Antichrist. He arose from the "sea." I believe the sea is a symbol for humanity (other Bible passages in which the sea symbolizes the human race or wicked humanity include Isaiah 17:12–13 and 57:20, Daniel 7:2–3, and Psalms 65:7 and 89:9).

Beginning in Revelation 13:11–12, John goes on to reveal another symbolic beast: "Then I saw a second beast, coming out of the earth. It had two horns like a lamb, but it spoke like a dragon. It exercised all the authority of the first beast on its behalf, and made the earth and its inhabitants worship the first beast, whose fatal wound had been healed."

The second beast coming out of the earth is the False Prophet. Though he is referred to symbolically as "the second beast" in Revelation 13, the False Prophet is mentioned by name in Revelation 16:13, 19:20, and 20:10. The False Prophet is the ultimate fulfillment of the prophetic warning of Jesus: "For false messiahs and false prophets will appear and perform great signs and wonders to deceive, if possible, even the elect" (Matthew 24:24).

What does it mean that the second beast, the False Prophet, came out of the earth? For now, we can only speculate. When this prophecy is fulfilled, many will remember these words and recognize the False Prophet for what he is—an instrument of deception, a puppet of Satan.

John describes the second beast as having power to perform miraculous signs on behalf of the beast in order to deceive "the inhabitants of the earth." This second beast orders the people to set up an image in honor of the first beast, the Antichrist.

This passage in Revelation conforms to the prophecy of Daniel 9:27, where the angel Gabriel tells Daniel that, in the middle of the seven years of the Tribulation, the Antichrist will put an end to sacrifices and offerings at the temple. An image will be raised up in the temple in honor of the Antichrist—"an abomination that causes desolation."

The second beast—the False Prophet—will miraculously breathe life into the image of the first beast, and will have power from Satan himself—power to cause the image of the Antichrist to move and speak. What will the image say? It will undoubtedly order that anyone who refuses to worship the image of the Antichrist be executed.

John goes on to say that the second beast, the False Prophet, "forced all people, great and small, rich and poor, free and slave, to receive a mark on their right hands or on their foreheads, so that they could not buy or sell unless they had the mark, which is the name of the beast or the number of its name" (Revelation 13:16–17).

Imagine if the government told you that you could not hold a job, operate a business, or buy food unless you had an indelible satanic mark stamped on your body. How would you survive?

How would you feed your family? You couldn't start a business or get a job. You couldn't collect unemployment insurance or a welfare check. You couldn't go to a religious charity for help—the only legal religion is worship of the Antichrist, so all other religions are outlawed.

John says that the second beast "had two horns like a lamb, but it spoke like a dragon." The False Prophet will have a false Christ-like appearance, the appearance of a lamb—but he will have the voice of a dragon and will speak the words of Satan. People will see him as a divine spiritual leader, and Muslims will mistake him for the prophet Isa, the Masîḥ—whom we know as Jesus the Messiah, the Lamb of God.

The False Prophet will force the people of the world to worship the Antichrist. He will perform false miracles by the power of Satan, calling down fire from the sky and convincing people everywhere, including across the Muslim world, that he performs these false wonders by the power of God, the power of Allah.

According to Islamic eschatology, Isa will assist the Mahdi in the same way the book of Revelation says the False Prophet will assist the Antichrist—and together, they will establish the global empire of the Antichrist, which Muslims will mistake for the global caliphate of the Mahdi.

The resemblance of the Mahdi to the Antichrist is thus clearly no coincidence. Satan knows every verse of the Bible and he inspired every verse of the Quran. He is preparing the Islamic world to recognize the Antichrist as the Mahdi and the False Prophet as Isa.

DON'T FEAR THE NUMBER

In 1988, President Ronald Reagan was preparing to leave the White House and return to private life. He and his wife, Nancy, purchased a home in the Bel Air neighborhood of Los Angeles. It was a beautiful, spacious home—but there was one thing wrong. It was located at 666 St. Cloud Road. He couldn't live in a home that bore the number of the mark of the Beast, so he had the city change the number to 668.[215]

In Revelation 13:18, we read, "This calls for wisdom. Let the person who has insight calculate the number of the beast, for it is the number of a man. That number is 666." This verse has baffled believers for centuries, the number 666 actually terrifying people who think that if 666 is the "number of the beast," then it must be an "unlucky" number.

Many people have tried to decode that number in order to identify the Antichrist, but I don't think the number 666 is a secret code. Let's think about it rationally. What is the biblical number that represents the perfection and completeness of God? Seven.

In Genesis 1–2, God creates the world in six days and rests on the seventh. In Exodus 20:8–11, God commands his people to keep the Sabbath—the seventh day—as a day of rest, holy to the Lord. In Joshua 6:3–15, the Israelites marched around Jericho once a day for six days, and then marched around the city seven times on the seventh day. In Revelation 1, we see symbols of seven stars, seven lampstands, and seven churches representing completeness. In Matthew 18:21–22, Jesus tells Peter that complete and perfect forgiveness involves forgiving not just seven times but seventy times seven.

Seven represents perfection. If anything seems perfect at first glance but is not of God, then it is not a perfect seven. What number falls short of seven? Six. The number six represents something false, something that deceives the eye but falls short of God's perfection.

Perfection—or deception? If the perfection of Jesus Christ is a seven, then six represents the deception of Satan. Six represents fallenness—the lying wickedness that pretends to be perfect. If the holy Trinity of God (the Father, Son, and Holy Spirit) may be symbolized as 777, then the unholy trinity of Satan, the Antichrist, and the False Prophet must be 666.

This, of course, is merely my opinion, and there are other possible explanations of 666. Someday, after all of these prophecies are fulfilled, we will know for certain what each symbol in Revelation means.

Please discard any superstitious fears about the number 666. If your name is written in the Book of Life, then you have nothing to fear from the Antichrist's deception or from God's judgment (see Revelation 3:5, 20:12, and Philippians 4:3). When we receive Jesus as our Lord and Savior, he writes our names in the Book of Life with his own indelible blood—and once written, your name cannot be erased from his Book.

Years ago, I preached about the Book of Life from Revelation. I later learned that a twelve-year-old girl in the audience had heard me say that the False Prophet would force people to receive the mark of the Beast. She also heard me say that, in Heaven, the name of Jesus will be inscribed on our foreheads (Revelation 22:4).

She went home, stood before a mirror, and wrote JESUS on her forehead. When her parents saw, they asked her why she had written it. The girl explained, "I never want the Antichrist to put his name on my forehead. I always want to belong to Jesus."

Let's follow this child's wise example. Let's write the name of Jesus on our foreheads and boldly proclaim the name of Jesus to the world.

11

"MECCA MUSLIMS" AND "MEDINA MUSLIMS"

Writer Daniel Nayeri was born in Iran. His mother, Sima, was a wealthy and respected doctor and his father a dentist. Sima was a devout Shia Muslim and a *sayyed* (literally, a "holy one"), meaning that she was a direct descendant of Muhammad.

In Iran, it is unthinkable that a sayyed would abandon Islam—yet that is exactly what Sima did. After hearing stories about Jesus, she fell in love with him, and her newfound love for Jesus demanded everything of her. Jesus meant more to her than her social standing, her medical career, and even life itself.

In Iran, it's a crime for a Muslim to convert to Christianity, punishable by death. Sima knew this, yet she openly proclaimed her Christian faith, and even hung a little cross necklace from the rearview mirror of her car. This prompted someone to leave an anonymous note on her windshield that read, "If we see this cross again, we will kill you." So Sima replaced the little cross with a *much bigger* cross, boldly defying the death threat.

Daniel recalled, "She could've lived quietly and saved everyone the heartaches that would come. If she had kept her head down."[216] But his mother couldn't live that way.

When Sima was caught giving help to an underground church, the Islamic government of Iran issued a *fatwa*—an official death sentence—against her. So Sima took Daniel and his sister Dina and fled in the dead of night, leaving Daniel's father behind (he wanted nothing to do with Sima's Christian faith).

For many months, Sima, Daniel, and Dina lived in refugee camps, first in Dubai and later in Italy. They had no money or possessions—Sima had barely escaped with her life and her children.

Finally, in 1990, when Daniel was eight years old, they reached America and settled in Edmond, Oklahoma. They had to learn a new language and adjust to a new culture with unfamiliar foods and strange customs. Being the only Persians their Oklahoman classmates had ever met, Daniel and Dina faced hostility, prejudice, and bullying at school.

Years later, Daniel recorded his bittersweet memories in his autobiographical novel *Everything Sad Is Untrue*. Published in 2020, the book went on to win top honors, including a Christopher Award and a Newbery Honor. Though the book is technically a novel, Nayeri says that the story is true, and only names and dialogue have been fictionalized. In the book, he describes his mother Sima's amazing faith in Jesus:

> She wanted everybody to have what she had, to be free, to realize that in other religions you have rules and codes and obligations to follow to earn good things, but all you had to do with Jesus was believe he was the one who died for you.
>
> And she believed. . . .
>
> [People ask,] "Okay, but why did she convert?" . . .
>
> But I don't have an answer for them.
>
> How can you explain why you believe anything? So I just say what my mom says when people ask her. . . . She says, "Because it's true."
>
> It's true and it's more valuable than seven million dollars in gold coins, and thousands of acres of Persian countryside, and ten years of education to get a medical degree, and all your family, and a home, and the best cream puffs of Jolfa, and even maybe your life.
>
> My mom wouldn't have made the trade otherwise. If you believe it's true, that there is a God and He wants you

> to believe in Him and He sent His Son to die for you—then it has to take over your life. It has to be worth more than everything else, because heaven's waiting on the other side.[217]

Daniel Nayeri's mother, Sima, treasured her relationship with Jesus. She treasured it all the more because it cost her everything she'd once had as a devout Muslim in Iran. The love of Jesus and the truth of Jesus are mightier than the sword of Islam.

Jesus is the Lord of history, the reason for our hope of Heaven. He is the Way, the Truth, and the Life. Because of Jesus, we are not afraid to live—and we are not afraid to die. Like Daniel's mother, Sima, we must live out the truth of the gospel without fear or compromise.

"LOVE YOUR ENEMIES"

Many people have the impression that Christianity and Islam have a lot in common—and, in a superficial sense, they do. After all, they are both monotheistic belief systems that trace their origins back to Abraham. Both religions claim that Jesus was a significant person in history. Both believe in the afterlife, in the final judgment, in prayer and morality and charity. Both the Bible and the Quran contain stories of Adam and Eve, the flood of Noah, and Moses.

Yet they offer completely different views of life and salvation. The Christian faith is rooted in love, forgiveness, and new life through a personal relationship with the God of the universe. The Christian faith sets you free from guilt, fear, and bondage to sin. Christianity does not impose itself on unwilling people. You are free to accept or reject Jesus, and there is no compulsion.

Islam, by contrast, is a religion of fear, punishment, and submission. The utopian ideal of Islam is a world in which everyone strictly obeys every tenet of Islam, with no separation between religion and state. The Islamic ideal of a political system is one in which the edicts of religion are enforced by the power of the state.

Under Islam, there is no tolerance for other religions—and why should there be? All other religions are false, so why would you tolerate falsehood? Islam offers no loving God, no assurance of forgiveness, no power over sin, no personal relationship with the remote and unknowable Allah, no freedom from guilt, no tolerance or freedom of any kind.

The Christian life, on the other hand, is uncomplicated and liberating. The essence of Christian living is summed up in two simple commandments, as Jesus himself said: "'Love the Lord your God with all your heart and with all your soul and with all your mind.' This is the first and greatest commandment. And the second is like it: 'Love your neighbor as yourself.' All the Law and the Prophets hang on these two commandments" (Matthew 22:37–40; see also Deuteronomy 6:5).

The fact that the Christian life is uncomplicated does not mean it is easy, however. The demands of Jesus can be very hard at times, such as when he tells us, "Love your enemies" (Matthew 5:44 and Luke 6:27). Christian love is *agape* love, a self-sacrificing love that is not an emotion but a decision of the will. You can't always have warm fuzzy feelings about other people, but you can *choose* to show kindness to your enemies—and that is a very hard thing to do.

Islam has no concept similar to *agape* love. To a Muslim, being kind to enemies would not be showing love but weakness. Islam, by its very name, by its very definition, is a demand for surrender and submission.

THE SINS OF CHRISTIAN HISTORY

Muslims cite the Crusades as one of the great sins of Christian history, and to this day radical Muslims refer to Christians (and sometimes to Americans and Westerners in general) as "Crusaders." Many Christians are baffled by this because they are not aware of crimes committed by the Crusaders.

The Crusades were religious wars supported by the Catholic popes during the Middle Ages. Some Crusades were aimed at reclaiming Jerusalem and the Holy Land from Muslim rule. After the Crusaders captured Jerusalem in 1099, they slaughtered many innocent men, women, and children, including many Muslims and Jews. The Crusaders who committed these atrocities were disobedient to the gospel and the teachings of Christ.

What is often left out of the discussion is that the Crusades began as an effort to defend Christian lands and people from Muslim invaders. Of course, this does not excuse the sins of the Crusaders, but anti-Christian critics often cite the history of the Crusades to vilify Christianity and Christians—and they often neglect to mention the Muslim invasions that provoked the Crusades.

In the first six centuries of Christian history, Christian missionaries and evangelists peacefully spread the gospel throughout the Roman Empire, from Spain and the British Isles to Carthage and Egypt, with Armenia declaring Christianity its state religion in AD 301. The gospel spread into Persia, Mesopotamia, Herat (Afghanistan), Samarkand (Uzbekistan), and all the way to the Malabar Coast in southern India.

Then, beginning in the seventh century, Islam came sweeping out of Arabia, into the Holy Land and Persia, across North Africa and into Spain, and pouring into Turkey and up into Eastern Europe. Whereas Christianity spread through persuasion and conversion, Islam spread through military conquest. The history of Islam is thus a history of warfare and enslavement.

Under the theocratic rule of Islam, submission to the Muslim ruler is equated with submission to Allah. Islam doesn't simply require *belief* in Allah; it demands *surrender and submission*, as the Quran itself states: "The wandering Arabs say: We believe. Say (unto them, O Muhammad): Ye believe not, but rather say 'We submit,' for the faith hath not yet entered into your hearts" (Quran 49:14).[218]

"MECCA MUSLIMS" AND "MEDINA MUSLIMS"

I want to say this very clearly: Islamists—Muslims who wish to impose Islamic law upon all of society—represent only a small fraction of the global Muslim population.

According to Ayaan Hirsi Ali of the Hoover Institution, about 10 to 15 percent of Muslims worldwide are Islamists. "Out of well over 1.6 billion [people], or 23 percent of the globe's population," she writes, "that implies more than 160 million individuals [are Islamists]. Based on survey data on attitudes toward Sharia in Muslim countries, total support for Islamist activities in the world is likely significantly higher than that estimate."[219]

If the proportion of Islamists in the Muslim world is as high as 25 percent, that means that there are 400 million Islamists in the world—and that's a troubling thought. But it would also mean that three-quarters of Muslims are tolerant people who want to live at peace with their neighbors, regardless of religious and cultural differences.

Ayaan Hirsi Ali, who was raised in a Muslim family in Somalia and is now a Christian, goes on to explain the facts about Islamism:

> Political Islam is not just a religion . . . ; it is also a political ideology, a legal order, and in many ways also a military doctrine associated with the campaigns of the Prophet Muhammad. Political Islam rejects any kind of distinction between religion and politics, mosque and state. Political Islam even rejects the modern state in favor of a caliphate. . . .
>
> Political Islam as an ideology has its foundation in Islamic doctrine. However, "Islam," "Islamism," and "Muslims" are distinct concepts. Not all Muslims are Islamists, let alone violent, but all Islamists—including those who use violence—are Muslims. I believe the religion of Islam itself is indeed capable of reformation, if only to distinguish it more clearly from the political ideology of Islamism. But that task of reform can only be carried out by Muslims.[220]

Ali has suggested two interesting terms to help differentiate between mainstream Muslims and the smaller subset of Islamists: "Mecca Muslims" and "Medina Muslims." These terms refer to two distinct phases of Muhammad's development of Islamic doctrines.

The first phase of Muhammad's mission was the Mecca period, from AD 610 to 622, during the early days when Muhammad was teaching his followers the basic principles of Islam—the Oneness of God (*Tawheed*), preparing for the afterlife, personal faith, and living a good moral life. Islamic scholars believe that this was when the shorter, more spiritual passages of the Quran were composed. During this time, Muhammad and his followers faced severe persecution from the tribes of Mecca, which forced them to migrate (*hijra*) to Medina.

The second phase of Muhammad's mission was the Medina period, from AD 622 to 632. In Medina, Muhammad and his followers established the first Islamic state, which included a system of laws, regulations, and instructions for governing an Islamic society. It was there that Muhammad probably developed the longer, more practical passages of the Quran, many of which deal with defending the Muslim religion by force. The Medina phase was focused on establishing an Islamic society and implementing Islamic principles in all aspects of life—including law, politics, and government.

So, while the vast majority of Muslims are "Mecca Muslims," at least 160 million (and probably millions more) are "Medina Muslims"—fundamentalists and Islamists who want to impose political Islam on the world. This doesn't mean they all support violence and terrorism. Most Islamists, in fact, probably favor using stealth strategies to gain political power over Western society.

These stealth strategies include partnering with the secular left and Progressives to elect Islamists to political office. They also include establishing strong Islamic communities in Western nations, such as EPIC City in Texas (see chapter 2).

THE STRATEGY OF *DAWA*

The most difficult problem Islamists pose to Western societies is *not* terrorism. It's the Islamists' strategy of *dawa*. This Arabic word literally means "invitation," and has traditionally been used to refer to proselytizing by persuasion. The principle of *dawa* comes from Quran 16:125: "Invite (all) to the Way of thy Lord with wisdom and beautiful preaching; and argue with them in ways that are best and most gracious: for thy Lord knoweth best, who have strayed from His Path, and who receive guidance."[221]

Westerners, especially Christians, might hear *dawa* defined as "invitation" and assume that *dawa* is the Islamic version of what Christians call "witnessing" or "evangelism." For Christians, witnessing is telling others what we believe and what God has done in our lives, and inviting them to receive Jesus. And for "Mecca Muslims," *dawa* truly *is* similar to Christian witnessing.

But among the Islamist "Medina Muslims"—especially the hardline sect known as the Salafis (fundamentalist Sunnis who embrace the Islamic beliefs and practices of the earliest Muslims)—the word *dawa* is defined differently. Nina Wiedl of the Hudson Institute observes that Salafis often translate *dawa* to mean not just "invitation" but rather "Islamic mission."

Wiedl explains, "For those thinkers that adhere to the broad-based Salafist ideology typical of the Muslim Brotherhood and related revivalist groups, *dawa* isn't simply a method for spreading a spiritual teaching or performing charitable works; it is also an inherently political activity, whose principal aim is Islamic reform and revival leading to the eventual establishment of an Islamic state."[222]

In other words, Islamist groups such as the Muslim Brotherhood believe their mission is to establish a global caliphate through subversion, deception, indoctrination, and recruitment—plus violence, if necessary. *Dawa* is a strategy for achieving Islam's political goals, and involves exploiting the freedoms of the West to subvert those freedoms.

Ayaan Hirs Ali observes that many Islamist groups in Western society have fooled Western governments by posing as "moderate Muslim" organizations that represent mainstream Muslim communities, and many have even received funding and official sponsorship from Western governments. Ali, however, lists a number of well-known organizations that pose as "moderate" but are working to undermine Western freedoms: The Council on American-Islamic Relations (CAIR), The Muslim Public Affairs Council (MPAC), The Islamic Society of North America (ISNA), The International Institute of Islamic Thought (IIIT), and The Islamic Society of Boston.[223]

She notes that the *dawa* strategy of some Islamist groups involves claiming to represent the views of all Muslims (to artificially inflate their power and influence), facilitating the "Islamization" of Western lands, infiltration of the government and education system, and exploiting the "diversity, equity, and inclusion" (DEI) mindset of the left to form alliances with Progressive groups (and eventually take them over).

Ali notes that Islamist groups have made inroads into many vulnerable communities and organizations, including African-American prison populations, the Women's March, and Black Lives Matter. Islamists have persuaded news organizations, such as the Associated Press, to adopt biased language rules that further the Islamists' goals. They have also lobbied the United Nations and many governments to adopt policies for combatting "Islamophobia," resulting in censorship and the punishment of free speech. These international efforts are being heavily funded by oil-rich Islamist regimes in Qatar, Saudi Arabia, and Kuwait.[224]

"IT'S EASY TO DIE FOR THE TRUTH"

In recent years, there has been a phenomenon in the Muslim world that has gone largely unreported: increasing numbers of Muslims are investigating the claims of Jesus Christ, asking questions and exchanging viewpoints with Christians. Many are embarrassed by the hatred and violence of Islamic terrorists, and believe the extremists bring dishonor upon the Muslim religion.

A few years ago, when the ISIS terror organization was at the height of its power in Iraq and Syria, I heard about a young woman, just eighteen years old, who was raised in Mecca, the birthplace of Muhammad. I'll call her Samar.

All her life, Samar had been immersed in the teachings and rituals of Islam, but then during her teen years, she began to question what she'd been taught. She was troubled by reports of killings and suicide bombings inflicted on the world by terrorists, and especially by ISIS. She wondered how Allah could be pleased with the torture and slaughter of innocent people.

She began investigating Christianity by watching THE KINGDOM SAT, the twenty-four-hour satellite channel of Leading The Way that beams Christian programming across the Muslim world. As she watched, Samar found herself attracted to the message of Jesus and his love. She had never heard of such love in Islam.

When Samar's parents learned that she was watching Christian TV, they blocked the channel from their satellite receiver. Samar secretly called the follow-up team of THE KINGDOM SAT and told the phone counselor that she would be killed if her family knew she was thinking of giving her life to Christ. "I'm not ready to die for a lie," she said. "I want to know for sure that Jesus is the Truth, as he claimed."

Over the next eight months, Samar continued to call the follow-up team. Finally, she was certain that Jesus was far more than a mere prophet, as the Quran said. She was convinced that Jesus is the Way, the Truth, and the Life—and she prayed to receive him as her Lord and Savior.

"Now I'm ready to die," she told the counselor. "It's easy to die for the truth."

The phone counselor was already moved to tears by her courage and faith—but then Samar said something even more startling: "I thank God for ISIS, because ISIS opened my eyes." The last I heard, Samar continues to be the Lord's ambassador in Mecca, the fortress of Islam.

God loves the Muslim people. I long for Muslims to come to the one true God and to his Son Jesus who died on the cross to save sinners. Many Muslims are already coming to know Christ as their Savior—and there is room in his Kingdom for many more.

12

SAVING OUR CIVILIZATION: AN ACTION AGENDA

On Monday, May 13, 1996, seventeen-year-old David Boim, a Jewish-American student from New York City, stood at a bus stop in Beit-El, a small West Bank village north of Jerusalem. David was a student at a *yeshiva* (an Orthodox Jewish college) in Beit-El. As he waited for the bus to Jerusalem, he chatted with friends.

At the same time, two heavily armed Hamas terrorists, Amjad Hinawi and Khalil Tawfiq al-Sharif, were driving around, looking for Israelis to kill. Spotting David and his friends at the bus stop, they opened fire, then raced off. David's friend, Yair Greenbaum, was struck in the chest and would later recover. But David Boim was shot in the head and killed.

Hinawi and Al-Sharif escaped and were shielded by the Palestinian Authority, the quasi-governmental Islamist group that exercises control in the West Bank. A year after killing David Boim, one of the terrorists, Al-Sharif, donned an explosive vest and blew himself up on a Jerusalem street. The blast killed five innocent people and wounded 192.

And here's a shocking truth: The guns, bullets, and bombs that Hamas terrorists have used to kill and maim thousands of people, including David Boim, were purchased with American money.

After David's murder, his parents sued the American organizations they believed were helping to fund Hamas terrorists. Among the defendants were the Holy Land Foundation for Relief and Development, the American Middle Eastern League for Palestine, the American Muslim Society, and other organizations and individuals.

Joyce and Stanley Boim won their lawsuit in 2004 and were awarded a judgment of $156 million. More than two decades later, the Boims have still not collected a dime. Joyce Boim explained, "The same organizations found guilty of providing material support to the terrorists quickly disbanded rather than comply with the court's ruling. . . . Many of the same terrorism supporters went on to play very similar roles in very similar organizations, only with different names."[225]

Jihad is being waged across Western society—and it is funded by organizations operating inside the United States. Our civilization is under attack by Islamists in both overt ways (terrorist attacks) and covert ways (stealth finance, deception, and infiltration).

What can we do to defend our civilization and our faith? Here's a slate of practical actions that you and I can take to make an important difference for the Lord Jesus and for our civilization.

BE BOLD IN YOUR WITNESS FOR THE TRUTH

God told Joshua, "Have I not commanded you? Be strong and courageous. Do not be afraid; do not be discouraged, for the Lord your God will be with you wherever you go" (Joshua 1:9). God gave Joshua this assurance as he commissioned him to lead the Israelites into the Promised Land. Joshua surely remembered these words as he repeatedly faced challenges from hostile enemies.

Let's claim this command for ourselves. Let's be strong and courageous in the Lord, ready at all times to speak God's truth, to defend our values, and to proclaim the love of Jesus wherever we go. In your workplace, at school board meetings, on your campus, and elsewhere, you may encounter secular leftists and Islamists who want to silence you and intimidate you by calling you an "Islamophobe." Don't get angry—but don't let them silence you either. Plant your feet on the firm foundation of God's truth and speak the truth in love.

Here are three Scripture-based ways you can become bolder and more confident in your witness for Jesus.

First, base your confidence on God, not yourself. Don't worry about what anyone thinks about you. Don't worry about your reputation. Don't worry about anyone calling you names or leveling false accusations against you. Forget about self-confidence—just practice your "God-confidence." Embrace your weaknesses and remember that God's power is "made perfect in weakness" (2 Corinthians 12:9). He is the one who equips you for the spiritual battle and enables you to "demolish arguments and every pretension that sets itself up against the knowledge of God" (2 Corinthians 10:4–5).

Second, realize that the outcome is up to God. Don't worry about how others will react or whether they will accept or reject God's truth. Just be obedient and leave the results to God. If people hate you for speaking the truth, remember the words of Jesus: "If the world hates you, keep in mind that it hated me first" (John 15:18). When people oppose your message, they may be under conviction from the Holy Spirit. When the Holy Spirit reveals sin in human hearts, some people respond with repentance—but others respond with resistance and hostility. Defiance and opposition are natural human responses to uncomfortable truths. Don't take their hostility personally.

Third, ask the Holy Spirit for wisdom and guidance. Boldness, according to the Bible, is a supernatural gift, not a natural ability. When you pray, the Holy Spirit will give you the power, love, and wisdom to conquer your fears. Welcome the interruptions in your schedule—the Muslim who needs help in the grocery aisle, the leftist student who wants to argue with you after class. Those interruptions may be divine appointments.

Pray for wisdom—then speak God's message, boldly and confidently.

GRACIOUSLY BUT FIRMLY EXPOSE THE IRRATIONALITY OF THE LEFT

UN Watch is a Geneva-based organization that reports on human-rights abuses and seeks to hold the United Nations to the principles of its charter. In August 2025, UN Watch released a troubling video of a speech given by Francesca Albanese, an Italian legal scholar who serves as UN Special Rapporteur on the Occupied Palestinian Territories. Her job is to report (supposedly in an honest and unbiased way) on the human-rights situation in those territories.

In the video, Francesca Albanese tells an audience in Sicily on August 8, 2025, "People continue to say, 'But Hamas, Hamas, Hamas!' I don't think people have any idea what Hamas is. . . . Hamas is a political force that won the elections in 2005 whether we like it or not. Those were called the most democratic elections. . . . Hamas put together a system of schools, public facilities, hospitals. It was simply the authority, as it was called in technical jargon, the de facto authority. So it is critical that you understand that when you think of Hamas, you should not necessarily think of cut-throats, people armed to the teeth, or fighters. It's not like that."[226]

Yes, Hamas has built schools and hospitals—with terrorist tunnel networks running under them. Should we call Hamas terrorists "cut-throats"? Well, they have boasted of cutting thousands of throats. Should we think of them as fighters, armed to the teeth? The 1988 Hamas founding covenant literally states, "Jihad is its path and death for the sake of Allah is the loftiest of its wishes,"[227] and they are clearly living up to those words.

Francesca Albanese's words are emblematic of the irrationality of secular-left thinking. This kind of gaslighting by the Progressive left is all the worse when it is spouted by a credentialed representative of the United Nations.

There's a popular misconception that transnational organizations—such as the UN or the World Health Organization—are selflessly devoted to serving humanity and are therefore above reproach. But many people in these organizations, like Francesca Albanese, are dedicated leftists and Socialists. Why do so many people grant credibility to transnational organizations like the UN and the World Health Organization—credibility they don't deserve and fail to live up to?

British journalist Melanie Phillips was a leftist in her early years, and she understands leftist thinking. "It's a kind of an article of faith on the left," she said, "that 'transnational' is good because it's like the brotherhood of man, whereas individual nations are bad because they're 'colonialist' if they're 'white' nations."[228]

In an interview with an Australian journalist, Phillips explained the ideology that underlies the irrationality of leftist thinking, using the example of the activist group Queers for Palestine. "Anyone with half a brain can see," she said, "that gay people in Gaza . . . are thrown off the tops of tall buildings."

How, then, can a group call itself Queers for Palestine? She explains, "The answer is intersectionality. It is this ideology which has gripped them as a way of thinking that cannot be challenged, that the world is divided into two groups, the *powerful* and the *powerless*. You are either in one group or the other. It's the idea that all human relationships are built on power."[229]

This is why leftists, Progressives, and Socialists worldwide have sided with Hamas. They see the Palestinians as the powerless side of the equation. In the irrational thinking of the left, powerlessness is the equivalent of being morally right. The powerless can do no wrong. This bizarre notion is not rooted in any moral principles but in Marxist ideology.

For decades, leftists have been portraying Hamas fighters as noble underdogs. But after Hamas launched its horrifying attack against Israel on October 7, 2023, leftists suddenly had a huge problem. Video evidence that Hamas terrorists *themselves* recorded on body cameras and phones showed these "noble underdogs" committing unspeakable torture and butchery, slaughtering babies and children, raping women, and more.

The secular leftists who had supported the cause of Hamas now faced a dilemma. They could either admit that the cause they had supported was evil, or they could—irrationally—deny the truth and continue to claim the terrorists are the good guys. Most chose irrationality and denial. They can't admit—even to themselves—that they have been wrong all along. To do so would destroy their image of themselves as morally superior people who only support righteous causes.

Leftists can't face the truth—but you and I must stand firmly for the truth. When leftists tell you that Western civilization is the source of all of humanity's ills, calmly reply that Western civilization has given us the rule of law, constitutional government, democracy, the Bill of Rights, scientific innovation, art and literature, institutions of higher learning, and the greatest global prosperity in human history.

When leftists tell you that Western civilization invented slavery, calmly reply, "No, slavery has existed since history began. But Western civilization gave us the abolition movement and people like William Wilberforce, Abraham Lincoln, Frederick Douglass, and Harriet Tubman who joined forces to end the institution of slavery."

Don't be intimidated. Calmly expose the irrationality of the left. Defend reason. Defend truth. And defend Western civilization, which—despite its flaws—has largely been shaped by Judeo-Christian values and biblical principles.

PROTECT YOUNG MINDS FROM INDOCTRINATION

In 2015, the mother of a seventh grader at a Tennessee middle school was shocked to learn that her child was required to write out the Five Pillars of Islam and recite the Muslim confession, the *Shahada*, which states, "There is no God but Allah, and Muhammad is his prophet." Appearing on Fox News, this mom, Brandee Porterfield, said that this assignment seemed to be "the state sponsoring religion in schools. . . . It does seem like it's indoctrination."[230]

In New Jersey in 2017, seventh graders in a class on world cultures were studying a unit on Islam. A mother, Libby Hilsenrath, was checking her son's homework when she learned that her son was required to watch a video that claimed that the Quran is a "perfect guide for humanity" and "Allah is the one God." It concluded with the statement, "May God help us all find the true faith, Islam." Students were also given worksheets with a link to a website that explains how to convert to Islam.[231]

I'm not opposed to schools teaching students about Islamic culture and beliefs. But we should all be opposed to classroom indoctrination. These are just two instances of classroom indoctrination in Islam that happened to make the news. Similar cases of indoctrination are occurring all the time in hundreds of schools—and most pass under the radar of parents and the media.

This indoctrination of our students involves not only Islamic proselytizing but indoctrination in an array of destructive ideas: radical race ideology, white collective guilt ideology, radical gender and transgender ideology, radical diversity-equity-and-inclusion ideology (DEI), Marxist victim-oppressor ideology, and anti-Western and anti-American revisionist history, to name a few.

Woodrow Wilson was a leader in the early Progressive movement. In a 1914 speech at Princeton, before Wilson was elected president of the United States, he declared, "I have often said that the use of a university is to make young gentlemen as unlike their fathers as possible." He openly declared his goal of indoctrinating young minds to reject the values of their parents—a radical education agenda that leftists and Progressives are still pursuing today.[232]

Right now, more than 10 million children in America attend schools where teachers and other employees are required to hide a student's "gender transition" from parents.[233] This means that if a child even expresses doubts about his or her gender, school employees must hide this information from the parents. Radical teachers sometimes coax impressionable children into confessing "doubts" about their sexuality—especially if a boy seems a little effeminate or a girl appears a bit tomboyish. Across America, many schools are quietly placing children on a conveyer belt to so-called gender-affirming care—and not a word is said to the parents.

The only surefire way to defend your children against these ideologies is by either homeschooling them or placing them in a biblically sound private Christian school. (I stress "biblically sound" because I have heard stories of private schools that unknowingly hired Progressive teachers or staff members who sneaked their ideologies into the classroom.)

Though I defend Christian homeschooling and Christian private schools, I know that these options require a huge investment of the parents' time and money, and many parents simply can't afford these options. So I applaud Christian families and Christian teachers who remain within the public school system and seek to protect children from radical indoctrination.

Whether your children are educated in a homeschool co-op, a private school, or a public school, there are steps you should take to protect them from indoctrination.

First, *pray daily for your children.* Pray with them in the morning before they go to school, pray for them during the day, and pray over their beds at night. Ask God to protect them physically, mentally, emotionally, and spiritually. Ask God to give them boldness to speak openly about Jesus. If you are a grandparent, pray daily for the souls of your grandchildren. Only God can perfectly protect your children and grandchildren against the attacks of Satan and the lies of this fallen world.

Second, *know what your children are being taught.* Attend every parent-teacher conference, every open house, every school board meeting. Ask questions. Talk to your kids about what they are learning (the dinner table is a perfect setting for these conversations). If a child tells you something troubling, avoid over-reacting or jumping to conclusions. Gather all the facts before you act. Affirm your child for being candid with you.

In June 2025, in the case of *Mahmoud v. Taylor*, the U.S. Supreme Court declared that parents have the right to opt their children out of any lessons on religion, sexual orientation, or other subjects that conflict with the family's religious beliefs.[234] You, therefore, have a constitutional right to opt your children out of secular-left indoctrination.

Third, *empower your children to be witnesses for Jesus at school.* Help them memorize evangelistic Scripture passages. Talk to them about witnessing. Encourage them to take training in personal evangelism. The following is a list of organizations that offer programs for training young people in how to naturally share their faith: Dare 2 Share, Child Evangelism Fellowship's Christian Youth in Action program, Youth for Christ, Word of Life—Student Fusion (with a focus on short-term mission trips), Cru (formerly Campus Crusade for Christ), InterVarsity Christian Fellowship, Fellowship of Christian Athletes, Evangelism Explosion's Changemakers program, and the Billy Graham School of Evangelism Online.

Fourth, *teach your children how to think for themselves.* Encourage them to ask questions. Teach them to respect all teachers, but to also be aware that some teachers may promote non-Christian values. Encourage them to tell you if a teacher seems to push an ideological or anti-Christian agenda.

The Lord has commissioned parents with the crucial role of instructing children and shaping their character and values. The Bible emphasizes continuous godly instruction in the home: "These commandments that I give you today are to be on your hearts. Impress them on your children. Talk about them when you sit at home and when you walk along the road, when you lie down and when you get up" (Deuteronomy 6:6–7).

Fifth, *join forces with other Christian parents and grandparents.* Don't try to fight these battles alone. Gather with other prayer-warrior parents and grandparents in a biblically grounded church. Keep each other informed about local, state, and federal issues that affect your children. Gather in person and keep in touch on social media. Pray together with like-minded parents and grandparents for the protection, salvation, and sanctification of the precious children in your care.

TREAT THE NEWS WITH HEALTHY SKEPTICISM

Whenever you take in news, remember that the so-called mainstream media or legacy media—Reuters, the AP, CNN, ABC, CBS, NBC, NPR, the BBC, *The New York Times, The Washington Post, The Guardian,* and so forth—are all part of the Omnicause, the Red-Green Alliance. The far-left media is fully allied with Hamas and other Islamist groups, no matter what crimes they commit. Why? Because the media shares the Islamists' hatred for Western civilization.

In July 2025, USAID (the United States Agency for International Development) conducted an internal analysis of waste and theft of food and medicines it had sent to Gaza. One key finding was that between October 2023 and May 2025, USAID found

156 instances of losses of $4.6 million of humanitarian aid—and none of USAID's distribution partners blamed Hamas for stealing the shipments.

Though Hamas is infamous for stealing aid shipments, USAID's partner agencies almost *never* report Hamas raids. Why is that? "UN agencies and NGOs," a USAID official explained, "are extremely reticent to report Hamas interference out of fear of violent retribution by Hamas." Yet Hamas was almost certainly responsible for most, if not all, of the losses.

Someone within USAID leaked a doctored version of the findings to Reuters, and Reuters falsely reported that USAID had "found no evidence of systematic theft by the Palestinian militant group Hamas." In other words, Reuters told the world that Hamas had been cleared of any suspicion. CNN, ABC News, and other legacy media repeated the false story and declared Hamas innocent of any wrongdoing.

Hamas pounced on the report to score a public relations triumph. Izzat al-Rishq of the Hamas political bureau released a statement claiming that the USAID confirmed that there was no theft by Hamas. According to reporter Jonas Du of The Free Press, Al-Rishq used the Reuters story to "to fuel accusations of starvation and genocide against the U.S. and Israel."[235]

These news outlets had to have known they were reporting lies. There are many news accounts and video recordings online showing various Hamas hijackings of humanitarian aid (see the Endnotes for links to those reports and videos).[236]

Over and over, the media has lied to us—about the origins of COVID, about the science about keeping schools closed during COVID, about practicing "transgender surgeries" on minor children, and yes, about Hamas. So approach any news headline with healthy skepticism. Seek news outlets with reputations for integrity.

Pay special attention to the way news outlets report on Christianity, Western civilization, and Islam. When a news site publishes biased or false reporting, look up its contact page or email address and, in a respectful tone, inform the editors of the facts. Let these news outlets know you are holding them accountable.

HOLD THE GOVERNMENT ACCOUNTABLE

People often think, "What can one person do? The government is too big, too distant, too impersonal for me to have any influence." But every citizen in a democracy has influence. Every citizen has a voice. We each have a duty to do whatever we can to impact our government for Christ and his Kingdom. Our involvement may take many forms, from prayer to voting to writing our representatives to attending town hall meetings to running for office.

Consider one form of involvement: attending school board meetings. School boards typically meet once a month, and may also call special meetings to address urgent business. To find out when your local board meets, check the school district website or call the district office. Imagine how you could help the children of your community if you informed yourself on local issues and spoke up at meetings—or if you got elected to the school board yourself.

There are many ways to have an influence on local government. For example, many communities have citizen advisory panels that give guidance to civic leaders on education, policing, public health, small businesses, homelessness, and zoning.

Democratic governments exist to serve the people. If we don't speak up and express our values, how will they make good decisions?

The word "democracy" comes from the Greek word *dēmos*, meaning "the people." But democracy involves more than just voting. Democracy is a dynamic process of choosing the direction of our society, and it thrives on active participation by the people. Every email, phone call, or town hall question is a factor in moving our society either toward or away from God's design for society. Every act of engagement, great or small, declares, "I am a follower of Christ and my voice matters."

So stay informed, then contact your elected representatives by phone, mail, or email. To learn how to contact your representatives in the United States, from local officials all the way to the president, visit https://www.usa.gov/elected-officials. In Great Britain, visit https://www.parliament.uk/get-involved/contact-an-mp-or-lord/contact-your-mp/ to find your member of Parliament. You can't contact the prime minister directly by email, but you can write to 10 Downing Street, London SW1A 2AA.

YOU ARE NOT ALONE

Here's a "secret" you probably already know: Many so-called public servants don't like to be held accountable. In fact, some try very hard to keep the people in the dark about what they are doing.

For example, as we saw in chapter 7, thousands of British girls have been assaulted by "rape gangs" of immigrant men, and the authorities and leftist media have covered up these crimes. The cover-up was exposed in July 2024 when a radical Muslim from an immigrant family killed three little girls at a party in Southport. That crime sparked an uprising of concerned parents—and suddenly the people of Great Britain realized they were not alone. In fact, *they were the majority*—and they realized they'd been lied to.

As Glenn Harlan Reynolds, professor of law at the University of Tennessee, observes:

> Britain's Labour government is in trouble: Its program of massive third-world immigration from places like Pakistan and Somalia is wildly, overwhelmingly unpopular. But that's not the real problem.
>
> The real problem is that despite the best efforts of Prime Minister Keir Starmer and his leftist captive media, Britons themselves have discovered just how unpopular it is . . . [because] the government has been policing speech about immigration.
>
> Any criticism of open borders, lax enforcement or—worst of all—immigrant crime has been punished as "racist" and "hate speech" by the Starmer regime.[237]

Why has Britain opened its borders to uncontrolled illegal immigration, much as the United States did during the Biden years? Conservative politician Liz Truss, who was prime minister during a time of political upheaval in 2022, says that leftist politicians *claim* they are defending human rights—but that claim is a smokescreen to cover up their real goal: British elites are importing an underclass of foreign workers to prop up a sagging economy.

Truss told an interviewer, "You just have to say no to more immigration and that means taking on the Treasury and the Bank of England because those are the people pursuing the high migration policies. They're saying the only way we're going to keep Britain afloat is . . . by importing more migrants. . . . They're saying that if you cut migration, the British economy will go bust. I've got news for them: The British economy is already going bust."[238]

The secular-left British government has allied itself with the Islamists, isolating British citizens to keep them silent and afraid. "The British establishment," writes Glenn Harlan Reynolds, "would have been better served to let its citizens debate the immigration question openly and fairly. It didn't do so because it knew it would lose such a debate. Instead, it foisted open borders on a nation that didn't want them, then tried to silence opposition."[239]

Whether you live in America or Great Britian or another Western democracy, don't let anyone make you feel isolated and alone. You have a voice. Speak up for children who can't speak for themselves. Speak up for Western values and Western civilization. Speak up for the gospel of Jesus Christ.

Don't be intimidated. Form alliances with other likeminded people. Encourage and embolden each other. Pray for each other. Jesus said, "Where two or three gather in my name, there am I with them" (Matthew 18:20). By standing with other Christian parents and grandparents, by praying together and working together, you invite God to move mountains.

Jesus also said, "You are the salt of the earth. . . . You are the light of the world" (Matthew 5:13–14). Salt is a preservative. Light reveals truth. Who is going to preserve and illuminate our civilization if you and I don't speak up?

Be the salt Jesus has called you to be. Be the light that proclaims God's truth. Pray in his name. Act in his name. Then watch God work his will through you.

EPILOGUE

MY PRAYER FOR ALL MUSLIMS

I gave my life to Christ when I was a teenager in Egypt. Most of our neighbors and most of my friends at school were Muslims. Since then, I have felt a burden to reach Muslims with the gospel.

In 1982, while I was working on my Ph.D. at Emory University, I visited a group of Islamist Egyptians who had banded together and called themselves Jihad. These young Islamists were radically committed to political Islam, and I sensed that if this group continued to attract followers, it could become a threat to the entire world. As it turned out, many of the men in that group later joined Al-Qaeda.

I told these young men that I wanted to study their beliefs and write my Ph.D. dissertation on them. Though they were suspicious of my motives, they allowed me to come and observe their meetings. They also made it clear that—for my own good—I had better write only what they told me to write. I took their threats seriously. I knew these were dangerous men.

The time I spent with among those jihadists was a scary experience. But it was also a challenge to my own faith. I have asked myself many times, "Am I as committed to conquering the world with the love of Christ as they are committed to conquering the world for Islam?"

Remember the Great Commission we received from our resurrected Lord: "All authority in heaven and on earth has been given to me. Therefore go and make disciples of all nations, baptizing them in the name of the Father and of the Son and of the Holy Spirit, and teaching them to obey everything I have commanded you.

And surely I am with you always, to the very end of the age" (Matthew 28:18–20).

Our Lord has commissioned us to share the good news with everyone around us—including Muslims. He calls us to make disciples of all nations. Our message to the world is clear: Jesus is the Way, the Truth, and the Life—and he is the only way to God the Father.

I encourage churches, prayer groups, and individual Christians to pray daily for Muslims—and to double their prayers during the month of Ramadan, the Islamic month of fasting. Ramadan does not have fixed starting and ending dates on our calendar, but is the ninth month of the Islamic lunar calendar. (The Islamic lunar year is 354 or 355 days long, so on our calendar Ramadan begins ten to twelve days earlier each year.)

Muslims believe that the Quran was given to Muhammad during Ramadan. They believe that evil spirits are bound during this month. As a result, nearly all Muslims, including those who are only nominally religious, faithfully observe the ritual prayers and fasting. For an entire month, Muslims fast from the first light of dawn until sunset, and do not eat or drink all day.

Muslims believe that Ramadan is divided into three parts: During the first ten days, Allah forgives sins. During the second ten days, Allah shows his mercy to faithful Muslims. During the third ten days, Allah offers deliverance from hell to all who perform the Ramadan fast and rituals well. Yet Muslims can never be sure whether Allah is pleased with their Ramadan observance.

Please pray that, during this special time of religious observance and religious fear, Muslims will see that their works are insufficient. Pray that God will make them realize that fasting can't make them sinless in the presence of a holy God.

My prayer for Muslims is that a spirit of conviction will sweep through the Muslim community around the world. I pray that Muslims will dream dreams about Jesus, the Son of God—as many Muslims are already experiencing. I pray that many Muslims will have caring Christian friends who will exemplify and share the love of Jesus with them.

That is my prayer for Muslims. I hope it will be your prayer too.

GOD'S HEART IS BROKEN FOR MUSLIMS

God is doing amazing things in the Muslim world. Our international ministry, Leading The Way, is part of the work he is doing. Every day, twenty-four hours a day, our Leading The Way studios send Christian television programming across the Muslim world, serving the most spiritually needy people on this suffering planet.

Let me tell you about one young man whose life was touched by Leading The Way. We'll call him Hakeem. He learned to read the Quran when he was just three and a half, and wanted to grow up to be just like his grandfather, an imam at a local mosque.

When Hakeem was eighteen, he was turning the radio dial and came across an Arabic-language Christian radio station. As a devout Muslim, he knew he shouldn't listen—but he couldn't bring himself to change the channel, so he listened to the rest of the broadcast. Afterward, he couldn't stop thinking about Jesus.

Night after night, Hakeem tuned to the Christian station and listen to the gospel story. Almost against his will, he found himself praying, "God, if you are really there, if Jesus is the truth, show me a sign!"

Then he heard the radio announcer speak the words of John 3:16: "For God so loved the world that he gave his one and only Son, that whoever believes in him shall not perish but have eternal life." Hakeem recognized those words as the sign he had prayed for. He went to his knees and prayed to receive Jesus as his Lord and Savior.

Hakeem's father learned he had become a Christian—and flew into a rage. The father beat the boy, then grabbed a gun and shot at him—but missed. Hakeem ran for his life. As he fled, he knew he could never return home. He was exiled from his family.

Hakeem wanted to share the gospel with the Muslims all around him—but it wasn't safe to talk about Jesus in his home country. It took time, but he eventually made his way to North America, where he was discipled in the Christian faith.

Once established in the faith, Hakeem became the North American follow-up coordinator for Leading The Way. Today, whenever

Muslims call with questions about Jesus, Hakeem is uniquely equipped to answer those questions and lead people to Jesus. He also connects new believers to Arabic-language churches.

I pray for many more Muslims to find Jesus. There are nearly four million Muslims in the United States[240]—and I pray they will have many Christian friends who are bold enough to share the good news with them. Across the Muslim world, and increasingly in the Western world, God is preparing the hearts of Muslims to respond to the gospel of Jesus Christ.

Many people assume that Muslims are unreachable, that their hearts are closed to the gospel—but that's not true. Many Muslims today are disillusioned and wracked by doubt about Islam. They hunger for truth, hope, and inner peace.

Please join me in praying for a great wave of conversions to sweep through the Muslim people, including Muslim immigrants in the Western world. God loves Muslim people. His heart is broken for them. We have the truth they need. If the heart of Jesus Christ beats within us, we must boldly share his good news with the Muslim people all around us.

THE MUSLIM NEXT DOOR

Who is the Muslim in your neighborhood? Who is the Muslim next door?

The majority of the Muslims you're likely to meet are mainstream Muslims, not Islamists. Let's always think of them as people Jesus loves, people Jesus died for. Exercise discernment, but extend Christian kindness and friendship. As much as anyone else in your life, Muslims need Jesus—not Isa, the prophet, but Jesus the loving Savior, the Son of God who bled and died on the cross for your sins and theirs.

When you meet Muslims at work, at school, or in social situations, greet them with openness and hospitality. Show that you are interested in them as people. Invite them over for coffee or a meal. Ask them about their traditions and their culture. If they are from another country, ask them about the land where they were born.

Be neighborly and build connections of trust that can lead in time to an opportunity to share the gospel.

Ask God to give you a heart full of Christ-like compassion for Muslim people. Ask God to open a door to the gospel and to convict people of their need of Jesus. Pray that God will send forth his Spirit to release those who are held captive by false beliefs. Many Muslims fear that leaving Islam will provoke Allah's wrath, so pray against the spirit of fear that keeps so many Muslims imprisoned.

Ask the Holy Spirit for wisdom and discernment. Ask the Spirit to help you to know what you should say—and what is better left unsaid.

An Islamic tract distributed by Muslim students on university campuses claims that Christians believe in three gods rather than one. Many Christian college students don't have a good response to that claim. Make sure you understand the biblical doctrine of the Trinity, which states that there is only one God, and yet there exists a mystical triune relationship between God the Father, God the Son, and God the Spirit. (For biblical support, see Matthew 28:19, 2 Corinthians 13:14, and 1 Peter 1:2.)

Arm yourself with Scripture. Memorize passages of the Bible so that you will be able to speak to Muslims about the love of Jesus Christ, the truth of God's Word, and the assurance of eternal life.

As you pray and study the Scriptures, you may also want to study the Muslim religion so you can be better informed about what Muslims believe. I recommend such books as *The Gospel for Muslims* by Thabiti Anyabwile, *What Every Christian Needs to Know About the Qur'an* by James White, and *Seeking Allah, Finding Jesus* by Nabeel Qureshi.

Remember, you don't have to be an expert on Islam to tell others what Jesus has done in your life. But if you have the time and interest, you may want to acquaint yourself with the Quran. You will find that the Quran portrays Jesus as a miracle worker who was born of a virgin, lived a sinless life, and even raised the dead. Muslims have great respect for Jesus, whom they regard as a prophet, but Islam also teaches that Jesus was not the Son of God and that he did not die on the cross.

If the subject of Islamists and terrorism comes up, and if it seems appropriate, tell your Muslim friend that you know that most Muslims don't support violence.

Be an attentive listener. Avoid criticizing Islam. Don't try to refute or debunk your friend's faith. Avoid getting into an argument about what we *don't* believe; instead, focus on the truths we *do* believe. Present your faith in a cheerful, positive way, with clarity and sincerity.

Speak enthusiastically about what God has done in your life. It's hard to argue with personal experience.

Talk candidly about the essential features of the Christian faith: the crucifixion, the death and burial of Jesus, and his resurrection. Don't water down the gospel to make it more palatable to your Muslim listener. If your Muslim friend tells you that the Bible has been corrupted (which is what Muslims have been taught), you can say, without arguing, that you have always found the Bible to be in complete harmony with itself.

GOD CHANGES HEARTS

In 1962, Dr. D. James Kennedy founded Evangelism Explosion, a ministry that equips Christians to share their faith. Yet, just ten years earlier, when Kennedy was in his twenties, he had no interest in spiritual things. He didn't attend church or pray or think about Jesus.

How did he go from being spiritually apathetic to being one of the great proponents of evangelism in such a short time? What caused such a profound change in his life?

Kennedy's transformation began late one Sunday morning when the clock radio by his bed woke him up. The powerful voice of a radio preacher thundered, "Suppose you were to die today and stand before God and he were to ask you, 'What right do you have to enter my heaven?', what would you say?"

That question struck home. Young Kennedy had no answer to that question. As he listened to the broadcast, he realized he needed to be saved. Soon afterwards, he received Jesus as his Lord and Savior.

D. James Kennedy went on to be an influential Bible teacher, author, and soul-winner.[241]

The question that shook him out of his spiritual apathy became a cornerstone of the Evangelism Explosion movement: "If you were to die today and God asked you, 'What right do you have to enter my heaven?', what would you say?" That is a good question to ask anyone—including Muslims. This question gives you an opening to share the hope that is within you.

Former Muslims have told me that, upon hearing the gospel for the first time, they felt great fear. They are afraid that they may have believed a falsehood in the past—and they are also afraid that what the Quran says is true and that they will go to Hell if they leave Islam.

Fear is the stronghold of every false religion. Our greatest weapon against that fear is earnest and persistent prayer.

If your Muslim friend refuses to listen to you, keep praying. God can change hearts through the power of prayer alone. Trust the Holy Spirit to water the seed you have planted in that person's life. The Spirit is the One who convicts. The Spirit is the One who opens the eyes of the blind. The Spirit is the One who points the way to Jesus.

Above all, don't be afraid. The Creator of the Universe goes with you. Love Muslim people with the love of Jesus. Be as patient and kind to them as your Lord Jesus has been to you.

If you do that, and leave the results to God, it will be enough.

NOTES

1 Bari Weiss, "Welcome to the Global Intifada," The Free Press, May 22, 2025, https://www.thefp.com/p/welcome-to-the-global-intifada; Mariam Wahba, "My Friend Yaron," The Free Press, May 22, 2025, https://www.thefp.com/p/my-friend-yaron.

2 Michael Biesecker and Jim Mustian, "Israeli Embassy staffers' alleged Killer Railed Against Gaza War Online, Protested at Emanuel's Home," Associated Press, May 24, 2025, https://abc7chicago.com/post/elias-rodriguez-washington-dc-shooting-suspect-posted-gaza-war-online-protested-chicago-mayor-rahm-emanuels-home/16532127/.

3 Olivia Petter, "Margaret Atwood says Greta Thunberg is the 'Joan of Arc' of Environmentalism," *The Independent*, November 7, 2019, https://www.the-independent.com/life-style/margaret-atwood-greta-thunberg-joan-of-arc-environmentalism-climate-change-a9188841.html; Lucy Diavolo, "Greta Thunberg Named Time Magazine's 2019 Person of the Year," *Teen Vogue*, December 11, 2019, https://www.teenvogue.com/story/greta-thunberg-time-magazine-2019-person-of-the-year.

4 *Jerusalem Post* Staff, "Greta Thunberg Labeled 'Antisemite of the Week' Amid Anti-Israel Activity," *The Jerusalem Post*, September 17, 2024, https://www.jpost.com/diaspora/antisemitism/article-820466; Clarence Page, "In the 'Omnicause,' Colliding Causes Can Defeat Each Other's Purposes," *The Fulcrum*, July 12, 2024, https://thefulcrum.us/civic-engagement-education/political-protest.

5 Jared Malsin and Dov Lieber, "Gaza-Bound Activist Boat With Greta Thunberg Intercepted, Boarded by Israel," *The Wall Street Journal*, June 9, 2025, https://www.wsj.com/world/middle-east/gaza-bound-activist-boat-with-greta-thunberg-on-board-intercepted-by-israel-f38dd031.

6 Adam Durbin and Sam Hancock, "Gaza Activists' Aid Boat with Greta Thunberg on Board Docks in Israel," BBC.com, June 9, 2025, https://www.bbc.com/news/live/clyg5x15n3zt.

7 Emanuel Fabian, "Katz: Thunberg and the Other Detained Flotilla Activists Refused to Watch Film of Hamas Atrocities on Oct. 7," *The Times of Israel*, June 10, 2025, https://www.timesofisrael.com/liveblog_entry/katz-detained-flotilla-activists-refused-to-watch-film-of-hamas-atrocities-on-oct-7/.

8 Caitlin Gibson, "Before Greta Thunberg Was a Global Icon, She Was a Tormented Child Who Refused to Eat or Speak," *Washington Post*, March 16, 2020, https://www.washingtonpost.com/lifestyle/on-parenting/before-greta-thunberg-was-a-global-icon-she-was-a-tormented-child-who-refused-to-eat-or-speak/2020/03/16/eea2967a-63a4-11ea-acca-80c22bbee96f_story.html.

9 Profile, Mom for Gliberty (@fakegreekgrill), X.com, https://x.com/fakegreekgrill/status/1716853019105497174. In a pinned post on X, dated October 24, 2023, Alysia Ames wrote, "It seems like where 'intersectionality' went wrong was assuming that anyone with any claim to oppression must be part of one omnicause + global warming for some reason." See also Symposium, "Alysia Ames on the Omnicause," hosted by Rob Tracinski, YouTube.com, May 25, 2024, https://www.youtube.com/watch?v=29hZyxr3vCQ.

10 Hadley Freeman, "Welcome to The Omnicause, the Fatberg of Activism," *The Jewish Chronicle*, June 17, 2024, https://www.thejc.com/opinion/welcome-to-the-omnicause-the-fatberg-of-activism-rw849dht.

11 Jack Khoury and Yaniv Kubovich, "Hamas Files Found by Israel in Gaza Detail Execution of Senior Member Accused of Being Gay," *Haaretz*, April 3, 2024, https://www.haaretz.com/middle-east-news/palestinians/2024-04-03/ty-article-magazine/.premium/hamas-files-found-by-israel-in-gaza-detail-execution-of-senior-member-accused-of-being-gay/0000018e-9e6d-d64e-afce-fffd62370000.

12 Emily Washburn, "Radical Feminists for Hamas?" Daily Citizen, August 22, 2024, https://dailycitizen.focusonthefamily.com/radical-feminists-for-hamas/.

13 Andy Kessler, "The 'Omnicause' Is Collapsing," *The Wall Street Journal*, June 23, 2024, https://www.wsj.com/opinion/the-omnicause-is-collapsing-protests-radicals-intersectionality-e4249f52.

14 Ray Lewis, "Pro-Palestine Protesters Interrupt Philadelphia Pride March: 'No Pride In Genocide,'" KATU-2 ABC, June 3, 2024, https://katu.com/news/nation-world/pro-palestine-protesters-interrupt-philadelphia-pride-march-no-pride-in-genocide-philly-pennsylvania-pride-month-june-israel-hamas-activism-lgbt-protest-nyc.

15 Marina Watts, "In Smithsonian Race Guidelines, Rational Thinking and Hard Work Are White Values," *Newsweek*, July 17, 2020, updated May 25, 2021, https://www.newsweek.com/smithsonian-race-guidelines-rational-thinking-hard-work-are-white-values-1518333.

16 Eli Lake, "The Ties That Bind Islamists and Progressives," The Free Press, August 6, 2025, https://www.thefp.com/p/the-ties-that-bind-islamists-and.

17 Jonah Goldberg, "Don't Call This Conservatism," American Enterprise Institute, May 12, 2025, https://www.aei.org/op-eds/dont-call-this-conservatism/.

18 Whittaker Chambers, *Witness* (New York: Random House, 1952), 499–500.

19 Alan Feuer, "Linda Sansour Is a Brooklyn Homegirl in a Hijab," *The New York Times*, August 7, 2015.

20 ADL Center on Extremism, "Students for Justice in Palestine (SJP)," Anti-Defamation League, August 9, 2024, https://www.adl.org/resources/backgrounder/students-justice-palestine-sjp.

21 Joanie Margulies, "Who Is Zohran Mamdani, NYC Democratic Mayoral Candidate with Anti-Israel Stances?" *The Jerusalem Post*, June 25, 2025, https://www.jpost.com/israel-news/article-858965.

22 Peter Pinedo and Andrew Mark Miller, "City-Run Grocery Stores, Defunding Police, Safe Injection Sites: What to Know About NYC's Next Potential Mayor," FoxNews.com, June 25, 2025, https://www.foxnews.com/politics/city-run-grocery-stores-defunding-police-safe-injection-sites-what-know-about-nycs-next-potential-mayor.

23 NBC News, *Meet the Press*, "Zohran Mamdani says, 'I Don't Think that We Should Have Billionaires': Full Interview," YouTube.com, June 29, 2025, https://www.youtube.com/watch?v=zczuvHEMH58.

24 *New York Post* Editorial Board, "Zohran Mamdani's 'No Billionaires' Dream Fits HIS Goal—to Make Us All Live in Equal Misery," *New York Post*, June 30, 2025, https://nypost.com/2025/06/30/opinion/zohran-mamdanis-dream-of-no-billionaires-fits-his-goal-make-everyone-live-equally-in-misery/.

25 Joanie Margulies, "Who is Zohran Mamdani, NYC Democratic Mayoral Candidate with Anti-Israel Stances?" *The Jerusalem Post*, June 25, 2025 / June 26, 2025, https://www.jpost.com/israel-news/article-858965.

26 Jon Levine, "Mamdani Supporters Celebrate Win with Cries of 'Globalize the Intifada,'" *Washington Free Beacon*, June 25, 2025, https://freebeacon.com/elections/mamdani-supporters-celebrate-win-with-cries-of-globalize-the-intifada/.

27 NBC News, *Meet the Press*, "Asked to Condemn the Phrase 'Globalize the Intifada,' Mamdani Says Mayors Shouldn't 'Police Speech,'" YouTube.com, June 29, 2025, https://www.youtube.com/watch?v=ggV2SeiGrVw.

28 Imtiaz Mahmood (@ImtiazMadmood), X.com, July 7, 2025, "Taqiyya is an Islamic practice that allows Muslims to lie . . . ," https://x.com/ImtiazMadmood/status/1942232134196076649. (According to one online source, Imtiaz Mahmood is "a Chief Engineer at Thome Oil & Gas based

in England. . . . On his X account, Mahmood identifies as an 'Atheist, freethinker' and claims to be 'exposing Islam layer by layer' to inform non-Muslims about the religion." Spotlight Hate, "Imtiaz Mahmood," SpotlightHate.com, 2025, https://spotlighthate.com/individual/imtiaz-mahmood/.)

29 Amjad Taha (@amjadt25), X.com, June 26, 2025, "When a Muslim Brotherhood influenced . . .," https://x.com/amjadt25/status/1938398658468475223?s=43.

30 Amjad Taha (@amjadt25), X.com, June 4, 2025, "Not every key fits every lock . . .," https://x.com/amjadt25/status/1930252309768057027.

31 Mary Harrington, "Why is Greta Wearing a Keffiyeh?" UnHerd.com, May 15, 2024, https://unherd.com/2024/05/why-is-greta-wearing-a-keffiyeh/?us.

32 Fox News, "Anti-Israel Protesters Can't Seem to Define 'From the River to the Sea,'" YouTube.com, April 24, 2024, https://www.youtube.com/watch?v=Lx8PQ5ktQPE.

33 American Jewish Committee, "From the River to the Sea," AJC.org, 2025, https://www.ajc.org/translatehate/From-the-River-to-the-Sea.

34 NDTV News Desk, "Watch: New York Students Admit They Have No Idea What They Are Protesting," NDTV World News, April 26, 2024, https://www.ndtv.com/world-news/pro-palestine-protests-in-us-watch-new-york-students-admit-they-have-no-idea-what-they-are-protesting-5526452.

35 David Propper, "Paterson Mayor Calls NJ City 'Capital of Palestine' in Ramadan Kickoff Remarks: '4th Holiest City in the World,'" *New York Post*, March 10, 2025, https://nypost.com/2025/03/10/us-news/paterson-mayor-calls-nj-city-capital-of-palestine-in-ramadan-remarks/; Hannan Adely, "Paterson Marks Milestone With Election of First Arab-American Mayor," NorthJersey.com, May 9, 2018, https://www.northjersey.com/story/news/passaic/paterson/2018/05/09/paterson-election-city-marks-milestone-first-arab-american-mayor/595936002/.

36 Joseph Feldman, "NJ Mayor: Paterson Is the Capital of Palestine in the United States of America," VIN News, March 9, 2025, https://vinnews.com/2025/03/09/nj-mayor-paterson-is-the-capital-of-palestine-in-the-united-states-of-america/.

37 Amil Imani, "Soft Jihad in America [on Tariq Ramadan]," *Campus Watch*, February 23, 2020, https://www.meforum.org/campus-watch/soft-jihad-in-america-on-tariq-ramadan.

38 Julia Preston, "Hearing for Muslim Barred from the U.S.," *The New York Times*, April 14, 2006, https://www.nytimes.com/2006/04/14/us/nationalspecial3/hearing-for-muslim-barred-by-us.html; Avi Yellin, "Obama Administration Lifts US Ban on Muslim Brotherhood Leader [on Tariq Ramadan],"

Campus Watch, January 22, 2010, https://www.meforum.org/campus-watch/obama-administration-lifts-us-ban-on-muslim; Janice Kephart, "Did the President Really Tell Us that Tariq Ramadan Will Not Be Subject to Future Intelligence Assessments?" Center for Immigration Studies, January 27, 2010, https://cis.org/Kephart/Did-President-Really-Tell-Us-Tariq-Ramadan-Will-Not-Be-Subject-Future-Intelligence.

39 Richard Adams and Angelique Chrisafis, "Oxford University places Tariq Ramadan on leave amid rape claims," *The Guardian*, November 7, 2017, https://www.theguardian.com/world/2017/nov/07/oxford-university-places-tariq-ramadan-on-leave-amid-claims; Yann Bouchez, "Tariq Ramadan visé par une cinquième mise en examen pour viol," *Le Monde*, October 23, 2020, https://www.lemonde.fr/societe/article/2020/10/23/tariq-ramadan-vise-par-une-cinquieme-mise-en-examen-pour-viol_6057081_3224.html; Agence France-Presse in Geneva, "Islamic Scholar Tariq Ramadan Guilty of Rape, Swiss Appeal Court Finds," *The Guardian*, September 10, 2024, https://www.theguardian.com/world/article/2024/sep/10/islamic-scholar-tariq-ramadan-guilty-of-swiss-appeal-court-find.

40 Sam Westrop, "Plano, Texas, Hands $1.2 Million to Radical Terror-Aligned Charities, Including Controversial EPIC City," Middle East Forum, June 5, 2025, https://www.meforum.org/fwi/fwi-research/fwi-government-funding-of-islamism/plano-tx-hands-1-2-million-of-taxpayers-money-to-radical-mosques-and-terror-supporting-charities.

41 America's Top 100 LLC, "Dan L. Cogdell: Criminal Defense Litigation, White-Collar Criminal Defense," America's Top 100 Criminal Defense Attorneys, 2025, https://www.top100criminaldefenseattorneys.com/listing/dan-l-cogdell/; Sam Westrop, "Plano, Texas, Hands $1.2 Million to Radical Terror-Aligned Charities, Including Controversial EPIC City," Middle East Forum, June 5, 2025, https://www.meforum.org/fwi/fwi-research/fwi-government-funding-of-islamism/plano-tx-hands-1-2-million-of-taxpayers-money-to-radical-mosques-and-terror-supporting-charities.

42 James Madison, *Federalist* 10 (1787), National Constitution Center, 2025, https://constitutioncenter.org/the-constitution/historic-document-library/detail/james-madison-federalist-10-1788.

43 Adrian Ashford and Nick Wooten, "Fact-check: What we know about plans for the Muslim-centric neighborhood EPIC City," *Dallas Morning News*, May 20, 2025, https://www.dallasnews.com/news/faith/2025/05/20/fact-check-what-we-know-about-plans-for-the-muslim-centric-neighborhood-epic-city/.

44 Ibid.

45 Ibid.

46 Pickthall Translation, from Abdullah Yusuf Ali, Marmaduke William Pickthall, M.H. Shakir, translators, *Three Translations of the Koran (Al-Qur'an) Side by Side*, Project Gutenberg, October 27, 2005, updated December 12, 2020, 004.034, https://www.gutenberg.org/cache/epub/16955/pg16955-images.html.

47 Cofer Luster, Criminal Defense Lawyers, "Is Domestic Violence a Felony in Texas?—Fort Worth, TX," CoferLuster.com, November 26, 2024, https://coferluster.com/blog/is-domestic-violence-a-felony-in-texas/.

48 Islamic Clarity, "Yasir Qadhi on #WifeBeating," YouTube.com, October 12, 2020, https://www.youtube.com/watch?v=5daSpeu861A.

49 Ibid.

50 Clare Lopez, "Texas: 'EPIC City,'" *Front Page*, June 11, 2025, https://www.frontpagemag.com/texas-epic-city/.

51 Onize Oduah, "Little Mogadishu on the Mississippi," *World*, October 24, 2019, https://wng.org/articles/little-mogadishu-on-the-mississippi-1617298219; Lopez, op cit.

52 Sarah Pulliam Bailey, "In the First Majority-Muslim U.S. City, Residents Tense About Its Future," *The Washington Post*, November 21, 2015, https://www.washingtonpost.com/national/for-the-first-majority-muslim-us-city-residents-tense-about-its-future/2015/11/21/45d0ea96-8a24-11e5-be39-0034bb576eee_story.html.

53 Michael Kransz, "Jewish Groups Urge Trump to Withdraw Michigan Mayor's U.S. Ambassador Nomination," MLive.com, April 2, 2025, https://www.mlive.com/politics/2025/04/jewish-groups-urge-trump-to-withdraw-michigan-mayors-us-ambassador-nomination.html; Lopez, op cit.

54 Steven Stalinsky, "Welcome to Dearborn, America's Jihad Capital," *The Wall Street Journal*, February 2, 2024, https://www.wsj.com/opinion/welcome-to-dearborn-americas-jihad-capital-pro-hamas-michigan-counterterrorism-a99dba38; Daniel Greenfield, "Dearborn Mayor Claims Exposing Hamas Support Is 'Islamophobic,'" Jewish News Syndicate, February 4, 2024, https://www.jns.org/dearborn-mayor-claims-exposing-hamas-support-is-islamophobic/.

55 Abdullah H. Hammoud, "I'm the Mayor of Dearborn, Mich., and My City Feels Betrayed," *The New York Times*, February 20, 2024, https://www.nytimes.com/2024/02/20/opinion/biden-dearborn-michigan-gaza.html.

56 Wikipedia community, "List of British Muslim Politicians," August 19, 2024, updated April 16, 2025, Wikipedia: The Free Encyclopedia, https://en.wikipedia.org/wiki/List_of_British_Muslim_politicians.

57 Census 2021, "Religion, England and Wales: Census 2021," Census 2021, November 29, 2022, https://www.ons.gov.uk/peoplepopulationandcommunity/culturalidentity/religion/bulletins/religionenglandandwales/census2021.

58 Fatima al-Kassab, "Why London's Muslim Mayor Needs the Same Security as the King," NPR.org, April 17, 2024, https://www.npr.org/2024/04/17/1244304019/london-mayor-sadiq-khan-muslim.

59 Birmingham City Council, "Lord Mayor of Birmingham, Councillor Zafar Iqbal MBE," Birmingham.gov.uk, May 27, 2025, https://www.birmingham.gov.uk/info/20158/lord_mayor/2939/lord_mayor_of_birmingham_councillor_zafar_iqbal_mbe.

60 Lucy Ashton, "City Names First Black, Hijab-Wearing Lord Mayor," May 19, 2025, BBC.com, https://www.bbc.com/news/articles/cx2q5v2x30ro.

61 Tahmina Saleem, "Mayor of Luton: Councillor Tahmina Saleem," Luton: Our Services, 2025, https://m.luton.gov.uk/Page/Show/Council_government_and_democracy/Local-democracy/Your%20local%20councillors/Pages/mayor-of-luton.aspx.

62 *Oldham Evening Chronicle* Staff, "Mayor of Oldham Returns for a Second Term," *Oldham Evening Chronicle*, May 23, 2024, https://www.oldham-chronicle.co.uk/news-features/139/main-news/156220/mayor-of-oldham-returns-for-a-second-term.

63 BBC South, "Oxford Swears in First Muslim Woman Lord Mayor," BBC.com, May 19, 2023, https://www.bbc.com/news/uk-england-oxfordshire-65646618. According to the government of the United Kingdom, "In 2024, the most common origin region of asylum seekers was Asia and the most common single nationality was Pakistani, followed by Afghan. In previous recent years, the Middle East was the most common origin region, with Syrian and Iranian the most common nationalities." See House of Commons, "Research Briefing: Asylum Statistics," UK Parliament, May 28, 2025, https://commonslibrary.parliament.uk/research-briefings/sn01403/#:~:text=Nationality%20of%20asylum%20seekers%20and,Iranian%20the%20most%20common%20nationalities.

64 @brieflybynewj, "UK MP Slammed for Condemning Hamas as Pro-Islamists Lash Out," YouTube.com, May 24, 2025, https://www.youtube.com/shorts/ZQcWUy6w28A.

65 Amjad Taha (@amjadt25), X.com, May 21, 2025, "Your British Parliament isn't just compromised. . .," https://x.com/amjadt25/status/1925191688286294383.

66 Breaking Battlegrounds, "These are Voters, Not Just Babies Being Born," Facebook post, May 10, 2025, https://www.facebook.com/watch/?v=1318001839303431. Note: The phrase transliterated *Kuntum khayra ummatin* is from the Quran, Surah al-Imran (3:110), meaning "You are the best of nations."

67 Ibid.

68 Conrad Hackett, Marcin Stonawski, Yunping Tong, Stephanie Kramer, Anne Shi, and Dalia Fahmy, "10. Religion in Europe," Pew Research Center, June 9, 2025, https://www.pewresearch.org/religion/2025/06/09/religion-in-europe/.

69 Elon Musk (@elonmusk), X.com, January 3, 2025, "Starmer was complicit . . .," https://x.com/elonmusk/status/1875150194909823085.

70 Mary Harrington, "Britain's Grooming Gang Shame," UnHerd, June 17, 2025, https://unherd.com/2025/06/labours-grooming-gang-shame/.

71 Ibid; Simon Cottee, "How Liberal Cringe Protected The Grooming Gangs," UnHerd, June 21, 2025, https://unherd.com/2025/06/how-liberal-cringe-protected-the-grooming-gangs/.

72 Harrington, op cit.

73 Cottee, op cit.

74 Ibid.

75 Lucy Thornton, "Dad of Rotherham Survivor Hits Out at 'Sickening and Atrocious Lack of Justice,'" *Daily Mirror*, June 23, 2022, https://www.mirror.co.uk/news/uk-news/dad-rotherham-survivor-hits-out-27304614; Charlie Peters, "Rotherham Police Accused of Preparing False Document after Father Arrested While Attempting to Rescue Daughter from Grooming Gangs," GB News, July 11, 2025, https://www.gbnews.com/news/rotherham-police-accused-false-arrest-document; Harrington, op cit.

76 Google Arts and Culture, "The British Mosque," artsandculture.google.com, no date, https://artsandculture.google.com/story/the-british-mosque/AQXh7n2wOBoHLg; David Torrance, *Sharia Law Courts in the UK* (A Briefing for Parliament), May 1, 2019, "2. Statistics on Sharia Councils," 7, https://researchbriefings.files.parliament.uk/documents/CDP-2019-0102/CDP-2019-0102.pdf.

77 Office for National Statistics, "Baby Names in England and Wales: 2023," ONS Statistical Bulletin, December 5, 2024, https://www.ons.gov.uk/peoplepopulationandcommunity/birthsdeathsandmarriages/livebirths/bulletins/babynamesenglandandwales/2023.

78 Council on Foreign Relations, "A Conversation With Adel al-Jubeir," with host Isobel Coleman, YouTube.com, September 26, 2018, https://www.youtube.com/watch?v=BeVLkBL8GC0.

79 Frannie Block and Jay Solomon, "How Qatar Bought America," The Free Press, May 13, 2025, https://www.thefp.com/p/how-qatar-bought-america; Kat Lonsdorf, "Trump Administration Officially Accepts Jet from Qatar for Use as Air Force One," National Public Radio (NPR.org), May 21, 2025, https://www.npr.org/2025/05/21/nx-s1-5406420/trump-accepts-qatar-plane-air-force-one.

80 Chuck Ross, "Swalwell Had Meetings With Qatari Charity Tied to Terrorist Groups," *Washington Free Beacon*, July 20, 2021, https://freebeacon.com/democrats/swalwell-met-with-qatari-charity-tied-to-terrorist-groups/; Amiri Diwan of the State of Qatar, "HH The Amir Receives Delegation of the US. Congress," Amiri Diwan website, October 11, 2020, https://www.diwan.gov.qa/briefing-room/news/receiving-guests/2020/october/11/hh-the-amir-receives-delegation-from-us-congress; Samuel Chamberlain, "Eric Swalwell Posed Shirtless During Pricey Paid-For Qatar Trip," *New York Post*, July 9, 2021, updated July 11, 2021, https://nypost.com/2021/07/09/eric-swalwell-posed-shirtless-during-pricey-paid-for-qatar-trip/.

81 Ross, op cit.

82 Aryn Baker, "Here's What Will Happen to Qatar's Billion Dollar Stadiums Now That the World Cup Is Over, *Time*, December 20, 2022, https://time.com/6242292/what-happens-to-qatar-world-cup-stadiums/.

83 Amnesty International, "Qatar: Abuse of World Cup Workers Exposed," Amnesty.org, March 31, 2016, https://www.amnesty.org/en/latest/press-release/2016/03/abuse-of-world-cup-workers-exposed/.

84 Ross, op cit.

85 Sarath K. Ganji, "How Qatar Became a World Leader in Sportswashing," *Journal of Democracy*, November 2022, https://www.journalofdemocracy.org/how-qatar-became-a-world-leader-in-sportswashing/.

86 Statista, "Share of Adults in Great Britain that Have a Favorable View of Qatar in October and December 2022," Statista.com, https://www.statista.com/statistics/1361550/opinion-qatar-before-after-world-cup/.

87 Yair Galily, "Beyond the Goalposts: Decoding Qatar's Soft Power Puzzle and Its Paradox," *Contemporary Review of the Middle East*, 2025, https://journals.sagepub.com/doi/10.1177/23477989251325622.

88 Arno Rosenfeld, "The Secret History and Uncertain Future of Students for Justice in Palestine," Forward.com, December 20, 2023, https://forward.com/news/574014/students-for-justice-in-palestine-history-operations-network-national-sjp/; Program on Extremism, George Washington University, "Hamas's Influence on US Campuses: A Study of Networks, Strategies, and Ideological Advocacy," GW Program on Extremism, November 20, 2024, https://extremism.gwu.edu/

hamass-influence-us-campuses-study-networks-strategies-and-ideological-advocacy; Talia Barnes, "Tear Down Censorship, Not Posters," TheFIRE.org, October 26, 2023, https://www.thefire.org/news/tear-down-censorship-not-posters.

89 ISGAP, "Follow The Money: Qatar and the Muslim Brotherhood Funding of Higher Education in the United States," ISGAP.org, 2025, https://isgap.org/follow-the-money/.

90 ISGAP, *Foreign Infiltration: Georgetown, Qatar, and the Muslim Brotherhood* (New York: The Institute for the Study of Global Antisemitism and Policy, 2025), 12, https://isgap.org/wp-content/uploads/2025/06/FTM-GEORGETOWN-REPORT-2025-05-23-1.pdf.

91 Block and Solomon, op cit; Bruce Hoffman (@hoffman_bruce), X.com, November 12, 2023, "And of course Hamas acquired this arsenal . . .," https://x.com/hoffman_bruce/status/1723686124609040534.

92 MEMRI, "Sheikha Moza, Mother Of Qatari Emir: Sinwar 'Will Live On'; Al-Jazeera Journalists, Qatari Influencers: Yahya Sinwar Is A Role Model And A Legendary Hero," Special Dispatch No. 11626, MEMRI.org, October 21, 2024, https://www.memri.org/reports/sheikha-moza-mother-qatari-emir-sinwar-will-live-al-jazeera-journalists-qatari-influencers.

93 Georgetown University Qatar, "Her Highness Attends Georgetown University in Qatar's 20 Year Anniversary Celebration," Georgetown University, April 17, 2025, https://www.qatar.georgetown.edu/her-highness-attends-georgetown-university-in-qatars-20-year-anniversary-celebration/; Block and Solomon, op cit.

94 ISGAP, *Cornell University's Ten Billion Dollar Sale: Soft Power, Qatar, The Muslim Brotherhood, and an Antisemitism Crisis on Campus* (New York: The Institute for the Study of Global Antisemitism, 2024), https://isgap.org/wp-content/uploads/2024/03/Cornell_Ten_Billion_Dollar.pdf, 2-32.

95 Frannie Block and Maya Sulkin, "Qatar and China Are Pouring Billions Into Elite American Universities," The Free Press, April 27, 2025, https://www.thefp.com/p/explosion-in-foreign-funding-for-american-universities.

96 Mark Schneider and Christopher Robinson, "The Scale of Foreign Investments in US Higher Education is Huge—but Mostly Unmeasured," American Enterprise Institute, February 03, 2025, https://www.aei.org/education/the-scale-of-foreign-investments-in-us-higher-education-is-huge-but-mostly-unmeasured/.

97 Ibid.

98 Block and Solomon, op cit.

99 Counter Jihad, "'An Explanatory Memorandum'—The Brotherhood's Plan," CounterJihad.com, no date, https://counterjihad.com/backgrounder/an-explanatory-memorandum-the-brotherhoods-plan/.

100 Program on Extremism, George Washington University, *Hamas's Influence on US Campuses: A Study of Networks, Strategies, and Ideological Advocacy* (Washington, DC: Program on Extremism at George Washington University, 2024), 5, https://extremism.gwu.edu/sites/g/files/zaxdzs5746/files/2024-11/Pamphlet_compressed.pdf.

101 Keir Simmons and Gabe Gutierrez, "Qatar Ends Mediation Efforts between Israel and Hamas, Citing Lack of Good-Faith Negotiations," NBC News, November 9, 2024, https://www.nbcnews.com/news/world/qatar-hamas-gaza-hostages-israel-war-ceasefire-rcna179332; Isabel Vincent and Benjamin Weinthal, "Hamas Leaders Worth Staggering $11B Revel in Luxury—While Gaza's People Suffer," *New York Post*, November 7, 2023, https://nypost.com/2023/11/07/news/hamas-leaders-worth-11bn-live-luxury-lives-in-qatar/; FDD, "While Gazans Suffer, Hamas Leaders Live in Luxury," Foundation for Defense of Democracies, January 13, 2024, https://www.fdd.org/analysis/2024/01/13/while-gazans-suffer-hamas-leaders-live-in-luxury/.

102 Block and Solomon, op cit.

103 Ohad Merlin, "Qatari Al-Jazeera TV Show Praises October Massacre, Hamas, Amid Ceasefire Mediation," *The Jerusalem Post*, January 26, 2025, https://www.jpost.com/middle-east/article-839296; FDD, "New Al Jazeera Program Reveals Coordinated Effort With Hamas To Reshape October 7 Narrative," Foundation for Defense of Democracies, February 14, 2025, https://www.fdd.org/analysis/2025/02/14/new-al-jazeera-program-reveals-coordinated-effort-with-hamas-to-reshape-october-7-narrative/.

104 The Media Line Staff, "Is Al Jazeera a Mouthpiece for Hamas?" The Media Line, January 30, 2025, https://themedialine.org/top-stories/is-al-jazeera-a-mouthpiece-for-hamas/.

105 Natalie Ecanow, "Al Jazeera Allegedly Using Bots to Spread Propaganda While Skirting U.S. Law," Foundation for Defense of Democracies, December 9, 2024, https://www.fdd.org/analysis/policy_briefs/2024/12/09/al-jazeera-allegedly-using-bots-to-spread-propaganda-while-skirting-u-s-law/.

106 Frannie and Solomon, op cit.

107 *New York Post*, "Rioters Bombard Police from Overpass—Hurling Rocks, Fireworks and Scooters," YouTube.com, June 9, 2024, https://www.youtube.com/watch?v=h4QX3woCmZg.

108 Deni Ellis Béchard and Dean Visser, "Thermal Runaway Explains Why Waymo Cars Burned So Completely in the Recent Los Angeles Protests," *Scientific American*, June 9, 2025, https://www.scientificamerican.com/article/why-the-waymo-car-fires-in-recent-los-angeles-protests-caused-the-robotaxis/.

109 Connor Stringer and Susie Coen, "LA Riots Backed by Pro-Hamas Activists Who Called for City to Burn," *Telegraph* (UK), June 12, 2025, https://www.telegraph.co.uk/us/news/2025/06/12/la-riots-backed-by-pro-hamas-activists-called-city-burn/.

110 Austin Williams, "LA Protests: Riot Gear Distributed by Masked Group Sparks Questions, FOX 11, June 9, 2025, FOX 11, https://www.foxla.com/news/la-protest-gear-distribution-guard-response.

111 Chaim Lax, "Unity of Fields: Meet the Anti-Israel Group Promoting Violence & Terrorism From Inside the U.S.," HonestReporting.com, June 26, 2025, https://honestreporting.com/unity-of-fields-meet-the-anti-israel-group-promoting-violence-terrorism-from-inside-the-u-s/.

112 Ibid.

113 Ambassador Dore Gold, "The Muslim Brotherhood and the Egyptian Crisis," Jerusalem Center for Security and Foreign Affairs, February 2, 2011, https://jcpa.org/article/the-muslim-brotherhood-and-the-egyptian-crisis/.

114 Lorenzo Vidino, "The Muslim Brotherhood in Holland," Investigative Project on Terrorism, April 6, 2007, https://www.investigativeproject.org/298/the-muslim-brotherhood-in-holland.

115 Al Jazeera and News Agencies, "Egypt Upholds Life Sentences for 10 Muslim Brotherhood Figures," Al Jazeera, July 12, 2021, https://www.aljazeera.com/news/2021/7/12/egypt-upholds-life-sentences-for-10-muslim-brotherhood-figures.

116 Jeffrey Goldberg, "What the Muslim Brotherhood Stands For," *The Atlantic*, January 31, 2011, https://www.theatlantic.com/international/archive/2011/01/what-the-muslim-brotherhood-stands-for/70502/; MEMRI, "Muslim Brotherhood Supreme Guide: 'The U.S. Is Now Experiencing the Beginning of Its End'; Improvement and Change in the Muslim World 'Can Only Be Attained Through Jihad and Sacrifice'," Special Dispatch No. 3274, MEMRI.org, October 6, 2010, https://www.memri.org/reports/muslim-brotherhood-supreme-guide-us-now-experiencing-beginning-its-end-improvement-and.

117 Louise Mensch, "Exclusive: France 'Suppressed Reports of Gruesome Torture' at Bataclan Massacre," HeatStreet.com, July 15, 2016, http://heatst.com/uk/exclusive-france-suppressed-news-of-gruesome-torture-at-bataclan-massacre/.

118 Judith Bergman, "Europe Is Not Israel," *Israel Hayom*, July 18, 2016, https://www.israelhayom.co.il/opinion/398281.

119 Fr. Mark A. Pilon, "Religious Blindness—and its Consequences for Europe," TheCatholicThing.org, July 27, 2016, https://www.thecatholicthing.org/2016/07/27/religious-blindness-and-its-consequences-for-europe/.

120 Ibid.

121 Besheer Mohamed, "New Estimates Show U.S. Muslim Population Continues to Grow," Pew Research, January 3, 2018, https://www.pewresearch.org/short-reads/2018/01/03/new-estimates-show-u-s-muslim-population-continues-to-grow/; Office for National Statistics, "Religion by Age and Sex, England and Wales: Census 2021," ONS, January 30, 2023, https://www.ons.gov.uk/peoplepopulationandcommunity/culturalidentity/religion/articles/religionbyageandsexenglandandwales/census2021.

122 John Newby, "Voting Equates to Community Vibrancy, Engagement," *Northwest Arkansas Democrat-Gazette*, March 27, 2024, https://hl.nwaonline.com/news/2024/mar/27/voting-equates-to-community-vibrancy-engagement/; Ben Klemens, "Social Norms and Voter Turnout," Brookings Institute, January 26, 2004, https://www.brookings.edu/articles/social-norms-and-voter-turnout/.

123 Vivian Song, "Macron Demands Action Against Threat of Islamist Extremism," *The Telegraph*, May 21, 2025, https://www.telegraph.co.uk/world-news/2025/05/21/macron-demands-action-against-threat-of-islamist-extremism/.

124 Farid Hafez, "State-Sponsored Islamophobia in France Encourages Violence," Al Jazeera, July 5, 2025, https://www.aljazeera.com/opinions/2025/7/5/state-sponsored-islamophobia-in-france-encourages-violence.

125 Georgios Samaras, "Battleground Europe: The Rise of Anti-Woke Movements and Their Threat to Democracy," *Frontiers in Political Science*, 3, May 9, 2025, https://www.frontiersin.org/journals/political-science/articles/10.3389/fpos.2025.1568816/full.

126 Joshua Arnold, "France Hallucinates a Palestinian State, while Israel Must Confront Reality," Washington Stand, July 26, 2025, https://washingtonstand.com/commentary/france-hallucinates-a-palestinian-state-while-israel-must-confront-reality.

127 Ailin Vilches Arguello, "Hamas Continues to Praise Western Countries for Recognizing Palestinian State," *The Algemeiner*, August 13, 2025, https://www.algemeiner.com/2025/08/13/hamas-continues-praise-western-countries-recognizing-palestinian-state/; FDD, "'Palestinian State is One of the Fruits of October 7': Emboldened Hamas Credits Its Violence for Gains as Released Hostage Video Spurs Outcry," Foundation for the Defense

of Democracy, August 3, 2025, https://www.fdd.org/analysis/2025/08/03/palestinian-state-is-one-of-the-fruits-of-october-7-emboldened-hamas-credits-its-violence-for-gains-as-released-hostage-video-spurs-outcry/; New South Wales Jewish Board of Deputies, "Recognition of a Palestinian State," NSWJBD.org.au, August 11, 2025, https://nswjbd.org.au/2025/08/11/recognition-of-a-palestinian-state/; Maariv and *Jerusalem Post* Staff, "Hamas Official Boasts Oct. 7 'Resistance' Revived Palestinian Statehood Push Around the Globe," Yahoo! News, August 2, 2025, https://www.yahoo.com/news/articles/hamas-official-claims-oct-7-233726865.html.

128 Al-Azhar University, "Islamic Studies Classes," Al-Azhar Classes, 2025, https://alazharclasses.com/islamic-studies-courses/; Al-Azhar University, "Quran Memorization Tool," Al-Azhar Classes, 2025, https://alazharclasses.com/quran-memorization-tool/; Tasneem Ragab, "Mastering Tajweed: Essential Rules for Correct Qur'an Recitation," Ijaazah Online Academy (affiliated with Al-Azhar University), June 15, 2022, https://ijaazah.com/tajweed-rules-holy-quran-practice-theory/.

129 Sir William Muir, *The Life of Mahomet: From Original Sources*, Third Edition (London: Smith, Elder, & Co., 1894), 20.

130 George Liska, *Expanding Realism: The Historical Dimension of World Politics*, Lanham, MD: Rowman & Littlefield, 1998), 170.

131 Pickthall Translation, op cit.

132 Exploring the Quran and the Bible, "Was the Quran Standardized by Uthman or Abd al-Malik?: Prof. Stephen Shoemaker," YouTube.com, February 27, 2023, https://www.youtube.com/watch?v=yjIwXjyxvw0&t=14s; Yasir Qadhi, "Why Did Uthman Burn the Quran?" YouTube.com, May 26, 2012, https://www.youtube.com/watch?v=zBxN3iwF9YE&t=245s.

133 Charisma Magazine, "The Mysterious World of Islam," MyCharisma.com, January 31, 2002, https://mycharisma.com/uncategorized/the-mysterious-world-of-islam/.

134 Hassan R. Hammoud, "Illiteracy in the Arab World," Institute for International Cooperation of the Deutscher Volkshochschul-Verband, no date, https://www.dvv-international.de/en/adult-education-and-development/editions/aed-662006/education-for-all-and-literacy/illiteracy-in-the-arab-world; IISc, "40% of Muslim World's Population Unable to Read or Write: Study," Indian Institute of Science, February 11, 2015, https://wgbis.ces.iisc.ac.in/biodiversity/sahyadri_enews/newsletter/Issue86/assets/NEWS/Doughnut.

135 Huda, "The Importance of the Arabic Language in Islam," Learn Religions, June 25, 2019, https://www.learnreligions.com/arabic-language-in-islam-2004035.

136 Al-Khair Foundation, "Letters from the Prophet (saw)," Al-Khair Foundation, no date, https://alkhair.org/letters-from-the-prophet/; Alzahraa K. Ahmed, "The Message: The Story of Islam, Directed by Mustapha al-Aqqad," The Met, July 3, 2012, https://www.metmuseum.org/exhibitions/listings/2012/byzantium-and-islam/blog/cultural-connections/posts/the-message. (Where the word "God" was used in quotations, I have changed it to "Allah" to avoid confusion.)

137 Juan Eduardo Campo, *Encyclopedia of Islam* [Facts on File Library of Religion and Mythology] (New York: Facts on File, 2009), 494.

138 Sunnah (The Hadith of the Prophet Muhammad at Your Fingertips), "23 Funerals (Al-Janaa'iz)," Sunnah.com, no date, https://sunnah.com/bukhari:1241.

139 Absolute Orthodoxy, "Part 4: Charlie Rose Interview with Ecumenical Patriarch Bartholomew," YouTube.com, April 17, 2010, https://www.youtube.com/watch?v=0RCKYCsAcqo&t=439s.

140 Sheela M. Ahmed, "Asmaul Husna," Alhiqma: A Muslim Souk, August 30, 2024, https://alhiqma.com.sg/blogs/blog/asmaul-husna-what-does-it-mean-in-the-quran.

141 E.M. Wherry, *A Comprehensive Commentary on the Quran* (Osnabrück, Germany: Otto Zeller Verlag, 1973), 36.

142 Mustafa Khattab, The Clear Quran, Quran 9:29, Quran.com, no date, https://quran.com/at-tawbah/29.

143 Pickthall Translation, op cit.

144 Ibid.

145 Shariah Editor, "7 Miracles of Prophet Jesus (peace be upon him)," About Islam, December 31, 2024, https://aboutislam.net/shariah/quran/quranic-stories/7-miracles-prophet-jesus-peace-upon/.

146 Pickthall Translation, op cit.

147 Ibid.

148 Sadakat Kadri, *Heaven on Earth: A Journey Through Sharia Law from the Deserts of Ancient Arabia to the Streets of the Modern Muslim World* (New York: Farrar, Straus and Giroux, 2012), 158-159.

149 Malise Ruthven, *A Fury for God: The Islamist Attack on America* (London: Granta Books, 2004), 75.

150 Sayyid Qutb ash-Shaheed, "The America I Have Seen: In the Scale of Human Values" (1951), https://www.cia.gov/library/abbottabad-compound/3F/3F56ACA473044436B4C1740F65D5C3B6_Sayyid_Qutb_-_The_America_I_Have_Seen.pdf.

151 Lawrence Wright, *The Looming Tower: Al-Qaeda and the Road to 9/11* (New York: Vintage, 2007), 35.

152 Robert Spencer, "Sayyid Qutb and the Virginia Five," *Front Page*, December 18, 2009, http://www.frontpagemag.com/2009/robert-spencer/sayyid-qutb-and-the-virginia-five-by-robert-spencer/.

153 Wright, 36.

154 Pickthall Translation, op cit.

155 Ibid.

156 Ibid.

157 Ibid.

158 Andrew Bernard, "Cruz Reintroduces Bill to Designate Muslim Brotherhood as Terrorists," Jewish News Service, July 16, 2025, https://www.jns.org/cruz-reintroduces-bill-to-designate-muslim-brotherhood-as-terrorists/.

159 Senator Ted Cruz, Press Release: "Sen. Cruz Introduces The Muslim Brotherhood Terrorist Designation Act," Senate.gov, July 16, 2025, https://www.cruz.senate.gov/newsroom/in-the-news/sen-cruz-introduces-the-muslim-brotherhood-terrorist-designation-act.

160 Melissa Langsam Braunstein, "Ted Cruz Renews Bid to Designate the Muslim Brotherhood a Terror Group," *Jewish Chronicle*, June 11, 2025, https://www.thejc.com/opinion/ted-cruz-renews-bid-to-designate-the-muslim-brotherhood-a-terror-group-hxbgdk1t.

161 Ayaan Hirsi Ali and Richard Dawkins, with moderator Freddie Sayers, "Richard Dawkins vs. Ayaan Hirsi Ali: The God Debate" (transcript), Unherd.com, June 3, 2024, https://unherd.com/watch-listen/the-god-debate/.

162 James Buchan, "Children of Empire," *The Guardian*, July 20, 2007, https://www.theguardian.com/books/2007/jul/21/historybooks.featuresreviews.

163 Center for Preventive Action, "Conflict in Yemen and the Red Sea," Global Conflict Tracker, March 26, 2025, https://www.cfr.org/global-conflict-tracker/conflict/war-yemen; Afrah Nasser, "The Thorny Relationship between Yemen's Government and the Southern Transitional Council," Arab Center Washington DC, May 3, 2023, https://arabcenterdc.org/resource/the-thorny-relationship-between-yemens-government-and-the-southern-transitional-council/.

164 Peter Hannaford, "Next Stop: Iran," *Washington Examiner*, January 16, 2006, https://www.washingtonexaminer.com/magazine/1513214/next-stop-iran/.

165 Council on Foreign Relations, "Instability in Afghanistan," Center for Preventive Action, February 12, 2025, https://www.cfr.org/global-conflict-tracker/conflict/war-afghanistan; USIP, "Tracking the Taliban's (Mis) Treatment of Women," United States Institute of Peace, January 14, 2025, https://www.usip.org/tracking-talibans-Mistreatment-women; UN Women,

"FAQs: Afghan Women Three Years after the Taliban Takeover," UNWomen.org, 12 August 2024, https://www.unwomen.org/en/articles/faqs/faqs-afghan-women-three-years-after-the-taliban-takeover.

166 Abu Amina Elias, "Hadith on Bid'ah: Every Innovation Is Misguidance in Hellfire," Daily Hadith Online: The Sunnah of Prophet Muhammad, February 16, 2014, https://www.abuaminaelias.com/dailyhadithonline/2014/02/16/every-bidah-is-misguidance-fire/.

167 Bernard Lewis, "The Middle East, Westernized Despite Itself," *Middle East Quarterly*, Spring 1996, https://www.meforum.org/middle-east-quarterly/the-middle-east-westernized-despite-itself.

168 Al Jazeera, "ISIL Video Shows Christian Egyptians Beheaded in Libya," Al Jazeera, February 16, 2015, https://www.aljazeera.com/news/2015/2/16/isil-video-shows-christian-egyptians-beheaded-in-libya; Stefan J. Bos, "African Man Turns To Christ Moments Before Beheading," Bos News Life, April 23, 2015, https://web.archive.org/web/20170825205726/http://www.bosnewslife.com/35141-african-man-turns-to-christ-moments-before-beheading.

169 Michael S. Smith II, "IS in Libya Threatens Rome," Inside the Jihad, February 15, 2015, https://insidethejihad.com/2015/02/is-in-libya-threatens-rome/.

170 Eliza Griswold, "Is This the End of Christianity in the Middle East?" *The New York Times*, July 22, 2015, https://www.nytimes.com/2015/07/26/magazine/is-this-the-end-of-christianity-in-the-middle-east.html.

171 Mufti A.H. Elias and Mohammad Ali ibn Zubair Ali, "Imam Mahdi (Descendent of Prophet Muhammad PBUH)," Islam.tc, http://www.islam.tc/prophecies/imam.html.

172 Andy Niklaus, Ulrich Rippert, "How the Verdi Union Wants to Prevent an Indefinite All-Out Transport Strike in Germany," World Socialist Web Site, February 29, 2024, https://www.wsws.org/en/articles/2024/03/01/inzb-m01.html.

173 Sabine Beppler-Spahl, "Don't Mention Islamism: Deflection and Moral Posturing Rule in Germany," The European Conservative, February 17, 2025, https://europeanconservative.com/articles/commentary/dont-mention-islamism-deflection-and-moral-posturing-rule-in-germany.

174 Ibid.

175 Pickthall Translation, op cit.

176 Quilliam Foundation, "Quilliam Exclusive—Translation and Analysis of Islamic State Document Highlighting Its Strategic Goals in Libya," February 18, 2015, http://www.quilliamfoundation.org/press/quilliam-

exclusive-translation-and-analysis-of-islamic-state-document-highlighting-its-strategic-goals-in-libya/; Charlie Winter, translator, *Libya: The Strategic Gateway for the Islamic State: Translation and Analysis of IS Recruitment Propaganda for Libya*, February 2015, Quilliam Foundation, http://www.quilliamfoundation.org/wp/wp-content/uploads/publications/free/libya-the-strategic-gateway-for-the-is.pdf. [Note: These resources are no longer available online. Quilliam was a British counter-extremism think tank founded in 2008 and closed in 2021.]

177 *Times of Israel* staff, "Breed and Conquer Europe, al-Aqsa Preacher Exhorts Muslims," *The Times of Israel*, September 19, 2015, http://www.timesofisrael.com/breed-and-conquer-europe-al-aqsa-preacher-exhorts-muslims/; MEMRI, "Al-Aqsa Mosque Address: Europe Wants the Muslim Refugees as Labor; We Shall Conquer Their Countries," Special Dispatch No. 5076, MEMRI.org, September 11, 2015, https://www.memri.org/tv/al-aqsa-mosque-address-europe-wants-muslim-refugees-labor-we-shall-conquer-their-countries.

178 Pew Research, "Europe's Growing Muslim Population," Pew Research Center, November 29, 2017, https://www.pewresearch.org/religion/2017/11/29/europes-growing-muslim-population/; Pew Research, "1. Demographic Portrait of Muslim Americans," Pew Research Center, July 26, 2017, https://www.pewresearch.org/religion/2017/07/26/demographic-portrait-of-muslim-americans/.

179 Abraham Lincoln, "Lyceum Address," January 27, 1838, from *Collected Works of Abraham Lincoln*, edited by Roy P. Basler et al., http://www.abrahamlincolnonline.org/lincoln/speeches/lyceum.htm.

180 Ronni L. Gordon and David M. Stillman, "Prince Charles of Arabia," *Middle East Quarterly*, Fall 1997, https://www.meforum.org/middle-east-quarterly/prince-charles-of-arabia; Daniel Pipes, "Is Prince Charles a Convert to Islam?" DanielPipes.org, September 13, 2022, https://www.danielpipes.org/blog/2003/01/is-prince-charles-a-convert-to-islam.

181 Tim Black, "The Islamophilia of King Charles," Spiked, July 22, 2025, https://www.spiked-online.com/2025/07/22/the-islamophilia-of-king-charles/.

182 Rayhan Uddin, "King Charles III: Five Things the New British Monarch Said about Islam and Muslims," Middle East Eye, September 13, 2022, https://www.middleeasteye.net/news/king-charles-iii-five-things-islam-muslims.

183 Ibid.

184 Gordon Rayner, "Prince Charles Takes Private Arabic Lessons," *The Telegraph*, March 14, 2013, https://www.telegraph.co.uk/news/uknews/prince-charles/9929142/Prince-Charles-takes-private-Arabic-lessons.html.

185 Liz Potter, "Highgrove: The King's Crowning Glory," Royal Horticultural Society, no date, https://www.rhs.org.uk/about-us/our-people/the-royal-family/Highgrove.

186 Peter Oborne and Imran Mulla, "Charles III: How the New King Became the Most Pro-Islam Monarch in British History," Middle East Eye, September 12, 2022, https://www.middleeasteye.net/opinion/king-charles-most-pro-islam-monarch-british-history.

187 Gabriel Pogrund, Charles Keidan, and Katherine Faulkner, "Prince Charles Accepted €1m Cash in Suitcase from Sheikh," *The Sunday Times*, June 25, 2022, https://www.thetimes.com/uk/royal-family/article/charles-accepted-1m-cash-in-suitcase-from-sheikh-j2pgnfsgx.

188 HRH The Prince of Wales, "Islam and the West," Speech at the Oxford Centre for Islamic Studies, October 27, 1993, posted by Furman University (Greenville, South Carolina), no date, https://eweb.furman.edu/~ateipen/pr_charles_speech.html.

189 Ibid.

190 Ibid.

191 Lucy Ballinger, "'Our chants weren't offensive,' Say Muslim Protesters Accused of Yelling Abuse at Soldiers' Homecoming Parade," *Daily Mail*, January 12, 2010, https://www.dailymail.co.uk/news/article-1241666/Our-chants-werent-offensive-say-Muslim-protesters-soldiers-homecoming-parade.html; Lucy Ballinger and Dan Newling, "Guilty? It's a Badge of Honour Say Muslim Hate Mob (And Because We're on Benefits, the State Will Pay Our Costs)," *Daily Mail*, January 12, 2010, https://www.dailymail.co.uk/news/article-1242335/Muslims-called-British-soldiers-rapists-cowards-scum-exercising-freedom-speech-court-hears.html.

192 Robert Johnson, "Muslim Preacher Tells Followers Getting Welfare Cash for Holy Wars is Easy and Right," *Business Insider*, February 18, 2013, https://www.businessinsider.com/anjem-choudary-muslim-preacher-explains-government-assistance-to-fund-jihad-holy-war-2013-2.

193 Dominic Casciani, "How Anjem Choudary's Mouth Was Finally Shut," BBC.com, August 16, 2016, https://www.bbc.com/news/magazine-36979892.

194 Ballinger and Newling, op cit.

195 Casciani, op cit.

196 David Ben-Basat, "Britain Faces a Test of Identity: Will Britons Become a Minority in Their Homeland?—Opinion," *The Jerusalem Post*, July 20, 2025, https://www.jpost.com/opinion/article-861437.

197 Ibid.

198 Hugh Fitzgerald, "Muslims and the Future of Britain," Jihad Watch, July 23, 2025, https://jihadwatch.org/2025/07/muslims-and-the-future-of-britain.

199 Ibid.

200 Dominic Green, "Are These Mothers Starting a Revolt in England?" The Free Press, August 4, 2025, https://www.thefp.com/p/are-these-mothers-starting-a-revolt-politics-international-europe.

201 Aletha Adu, "Starmer: I'm a Socialist And Progressive Who Will Always Put Country First," *The Guardian*, May 27, 2024, https://www.theguardian.com/politics/article/2024/may/27/starmer-im-a-socialist-and-progressive-who-will-always-put-country-first.

202 Dominic Green, "Blasphemy Laws and Two-Tiered Policing Arrive in Britain," The Free Press, June 3, 2025, https://www.thefp.com/p/the-british-mother-serving-time-for; Green, "Are These Mothers . . .," op cit.; Lewis Adams, "Man Tried to Kiss Schoolgirl, Court Told," BBC News Essex, July 17, 2025, https://www.bbc.com/news/articles/c9qx-2qedqllo; Laurie Wastell, "The People of Epping Are Fed Up with Being Ignored," *Spectator*, July 19, 2025, https://www.spectator.co.uk/article/the-people-of-epping-are-fed-up-of-being-ignored/.

203 Translation of Sahih Muslim, Book 41: Kitab Al-Fitan Wa Ashrat As-Sa'ah (Book Pertaining To The Turmoil And Portents Of The Last Hour), Book 41, Number 6924, https://m.iium.edu.my/deed/hadith/muslim/041_smt.html.

204 Salma Abdelaziz, "ISIS States Its Justification for the Enslavement of Women," CNN.com, October 13, 2014, https://www.cnn.com/2014/10/12/world/meast/isis-justification-slavery/.

205 BBC Monitoring, "Dabiq: Why Is Syrian Town So Important for IS?" BBC.com, October 4, 2016, https://www.bbc.com/news/world-middle-east-30083303; Rudaw staff, "Turkey Reports Killing 47 ISIS Militants in Syria in One Day," Rudaw.net, December 10, 2016, https://www.rudaw.net/english/middleeast/turkey/121020161.

206 Ben Wedeman and Lauren Said-Moorhouse, "ISIS Has Lost Its Final Stronghold in Syria, the Syrian Democratic Forces Says," CNN.com, March 23, 2019, https://www.cnn.com/2019/03/23/middleeast/isis-caliphate-end-intl; Richard Gonzales, "Head of U.S. Central Command Says ISIS Leader Baghdadi Buried at Sea," NPR.org, October 30, 2019, https://www.npr.org/2019/10/30/774617578/head-of-u-s-central-command-says-isis-leader-baghdadi-buried-at-sea.

207 Shaykh Muhammad Hisham Kabbani, *The Approach of Armageddon? An Islamic Perspective* (Washington DC, Supreme Muslim Council of America, 2003), 229.

208 Samuel Shahid, *The Last Trumpet: A Comparative Study in Christian-Islamic Eschatology* (Camarillo, CA: Xulon, 2005), 114, 119–20.

209 Muhammad Ibn Izzat and Muhammad Arif, *Al Mahdi and the End of Time* (London, Dar al-Taqwa, 1997), 40–41.

210 Ibrahim Amini, *Al-Imam al-Mahdi, The Just Leader of Humanity*, translated by Abdulaziz Sachedina (Qum, Iran: Ansariyan Publications, no date), PDF version, http://www.al-islam.org/printpdf/book/export/html/13072.

211 Shihab al-Din Mujtahidi, "Imam Mahdi, the Universal Leader," ShariaStudies.com, January 25, 2020, https://shiastudies.com/en/2423/imam-mahdi-the-universal-leader/.

212 AskIslamPedia, "Imaam Mahdi and the Signs that Will Precede Him," AskIslamPedia.com, no date, https://www.askislampedia.com/wiki/-/wiki/English_wiki/Imaam+Mahdi+and+the+Signs+that+Will+Precede+Him/.

213 Ibn Izzat and Arif, 15.

214 Kabbani, 231.

215 Ching-Ching Ni, "In Arcadia Real Estate, 4 Is A Negative Number," *Los Angeles Times*, May 21, 2011, https://www.latimes.com/local/la-xpm-2011-may-21-la-me-arcadia-numbers-20110521-story.html.

216 Daniel Nayeri, *Everything Sad Is Untrue* (New York: Levine Quierido, 2020), 206–207.

217 Nayeri, 196–197.

218 Pickthall Translation, op cit.

219 Ayaan Hirsi Ali, "How to Counter Political Islam," Hoover Institution, March 22, 2017, https://www.hoover.org/research/how-counter-political-islam.

220 Ibid.

221 Pickthall Translation, op cit.

222 Nina Wiedl, "Dawa and the Islamist Revival in the West," Hudson Institute, December 14, 2009, https://www.hudson.org/national-security-defense/dawa-and-the-islamist-revival-in-the-west.

223 Ali, op cit.

224 Ibid.

225 Joyce Boim, "My Son Was One of the First Americans Killed by Hamas," *Tablet*, July 22, 2024, https://www.tabletmag.com/sections/news/articles/son-first-american-killed-hamas-david-boim; Matthew Kassel, "Boim Lawsuit Targets American Muslims for Palestine's Hamas Ties," *Jewish Insider*, April 23, 2025, https://jewishinsider.com/2025/04/david-boim-hamas-terrorists-lawsuit-american-muslims-for-palestine/; United States Court of Appeals for the Seventh Circuit, STANLEY BOIM, individually and as administrator of the ESTATE OF DAVID BOIM, deceased,

and JOYCE BOIM, Plaintiffs-Appellees, v. HOLY LAND FOUNDATION FOR RELIEF AND DEVELOPMENT, et al., Defendants-Appellants, https://uniset.ca/other/cs5/511F3d707.html.

226 UN Watch, "'Hamas, Hamas, Hamas:' UN's Terror Apologist Doubles Down," YouTube.com, August 15, 2025, https://www.youtube.com/watch?v=iRGhSjaB5UM&t=19s.

227 The Avalon Project, "Hamas Covenant 1988: The Covenant of the Islamic Resistance Movement," adopted August 18, 1988, Yale Law School, Lillian Goldman Law Library, posted 2008, https://avalon.law.yale.edu/20th_century/hamas.asp.

228 *The Erin Molan Show*, "She went Viral EXPOSING the Left; Now Melanie Phillips DESTROYS The UN," YouTube.com, August 18, 2025, https://www.youtube.com/watch?v=B_Za0e3mtVg.

229 Ibid.

230 Beth Greenfield, "School's Islam Lessons Freak Parents Out," Yahoo! News, September 9, 2015, https://www.yahoo.com/lifestyle/schools-islam-lessons-freak-parents-out-128717093772.html.

231 Deena Mousa, "Schools Teach About Islam—and Are Accused of Indoctrination," *Christian Science Monitor*, February 20, 2021, https://www.csmonitor.com/Commentary/2021/0219/Schools-teach-about-Islam-and-are-accused-of-indoctrination.

232 Dennis Prager, "Conservative Parents, Left-Wing Children," *National Review*, November 5, 2013, https://www.nationalreview.com/2013/11/conservative-parents-left-wing-children-dennis-prager/.

233 Michael Torres, "Whether You Like It Or Not," *City Journal*, July 18, 2023, https://www.city-journal.org/article/transgender-secrecy-policies-at-public-schools.

234 Thomas Peele, "California Schools Brace for Fallout from U.S. Supreme Court Decision on Religious Rights," EdSource.org, August 25, 2025, https://edsource.org/2025/alternatives-public-school-education/739199; MAHMOUD ET AL. v. TAYLOR ET AL., No. 24–297, Argued April 22, 2025, Decided June 27, 2025, https://www.supremecourt.gov/opinions/24pdf/24-297_4f14.pdf.

235 Jonas Du, "Why Is Reuters Carrying Water for Hamas?" The Free Press, August 11, 2025, https://www.thefp.com/p/why-is-reuters-carrying-water-for-hamas.

236 JNS Staff, "Hamas Caught on Film Stealing Gaza Aid, Again," Jewish News Service, October 10, 2024, https://www.jns.org/hamas-caught-on-film-stealing-gaza-aid-again/; @shiezoli, "Hamas terrorists Hijack Aid

Trucks in Gaza," YouTube.com, August 2, 2025, https://www.youtube.com/shorts/k9QcUyZQtfs; Israel Defense Forces, "This is How Hamas Steals Humanitarian Aid from Gazan Civilians," YouTube.com, February 7, 2024, https://www.youtube.com/watch?v=2DE3Xg2It-I; LiveNOW from FOX, "WATCH: Terrorist Killed While Attempting to Hijack Aid Truck in Gaza, IDF Says," YouTube.com, September 21, 2024, https://www.youtube.com/watch?v=cWNg_H76X5k; *The Sun*, "IDF Releases Footage of Hamas Beating Civilians and Stealing Aid in Gaza Strip," YouTube.com, December 12, 2023, https://www.youtube.com/watch?v=LnVST02SFfc.

237 Glenn H. Reynolds, "The Dam Is Breaking On Britain's Illegal Immigration Crisis—And The Results Could Be Ugly," *New York Post*, August 5, 2025, https://nypost.com/2025/08/05/opinion/uk-is-facing-migrant-crisis-reality-and-results-will-be-ugly/.

238 Ben Shapiro, "The Decline of the UK: Ben Shapiro & Fmr. UK PM Liz Truss," YouTube.com, August 11, 2025, https://www.youtube.com/watch?v=G7g5tNJtaoY.

239 Reynolds, op cit.

240 Veera Korhonen, "Muslims in the United States—Statistics & Facts," Statista, July 8, 2025, https://www.statista.com/topics/13415/muslims-in-the-united-states/.

241 Preaching.com Staff, "Dr. D. James Kennedy Dies," Preaching.com, September 2007, https://www.preaching.com/articles/dr-d-james-kennedy-dies/.

Passionately Proclaiming Uncompromising Truth

Truth You Can Trust. Truth That Transforms.

Follow *Leading The Way* for bold Biblical Truth, cultural clarity, frontline ministry updates, and timely encouragement from God's Word.

LTW.org

You'll Love These Other Books from Dr. Michael A. Youssef

Hope for This Present Crisis
A seven-step plan for cultural renewal

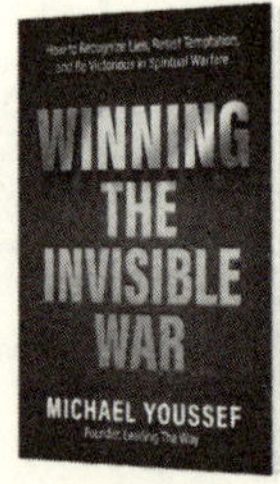

Winning the Invisible War
How to stand firm in unseen spiritual battles

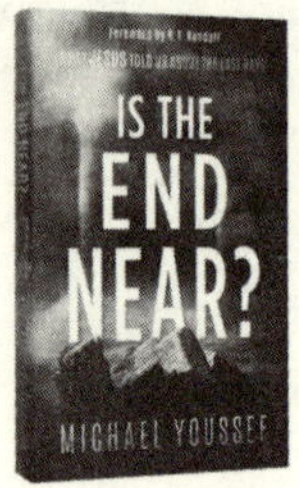

Is the End Near?
What Bible prophecy reveals about today's headlines

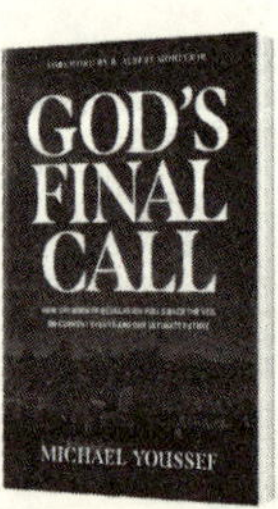

God's Final Call
A powerful wake-up call to the Church today

Saving Christianity?
The heresy weakening the Church—and the way forward